ALSO BY *Jean-Paul Sartre*

Drama

NO EXIT *and* THE FLIES

Fiction

ROADS TO FREEDOM (*Chemins de la liberté*)

Vol. I THE AGE OF REASON (*L'Âge de raison*)

Vol. II THE REPRIEVE (*Le Sursis*)

Vol. III *La Mort dans l'âme* (IN PREPARATION)

THESE ARE *Borzoi Books,*

PUBLISHED BY *Alfred A. Knopf* IN NEW YORK

Three Plays

Dirty Hands

(Les Mains sales)

A PLAY IN SEVEN ACTS

The Respectful Prostitute

(La Putain respectueuse)

A PLAY IN ONE ACT

The Victors

(Morts sans sépulture)

A PLAY IN FOUR ACTS

THREE PLAYS

BY

Jean-Paul Sartre

Translated from the French by LIONEL ABEL

1949 *ALFRED A. KNOPF New York*

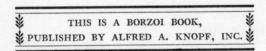

CONTENTS

DIRTY HANDS
(*Les Mains sales*)

A PLAY IN SEVEN ACTS

❖❖❖

To Dolorès

CHARACTERS IN THE PLAY

OLGA

HUGO

CHARLES

FRANTZ

LOUIS

IVAN

JESSICA

SLICK

GEORGE

HŒDERER

KARSKY

PRINCE PAUL

Les Mains sales (*Dirty Hands*) was presented for the first time at the Théâtre Antoine, Paris, on April 2, 1948.

DIRTY HANDS

A C T   I

OLGA'S HOUSE

The ground floor of a small cottage along the highway. To the right, the front door of the house and a window with the blinds drawn. To the rear, a telephone on a chest of drawers. To the left rear, a door. Tables, chairs. Oddly assorted pieces, all of cheap make. It is evident that the tenant is totally indifferent to furnishings. To the left, next to the door, a fireplace; above the fireplace, a mirror. Cars can be heard from time to time going up the road. Motor horns.

OLGA, *alone, is sitting by the radio, turning the dial. Confused sounds and then a clear voice:*

SPEAKER : The German armies are in full retreat all along the front. The Soviet armies have taken Kischnar, some twenty-five miles from the Illyrian frontier. Wherever possible, the Illyrian troops are refusing to fight; many deserters have already gone over to the Allies. Illyrians, we know that you were forced to take up arms against the U.S.S.R.; we are fully aware of the profoundly democratic sentiments of the people of Illyria, and we . . .

[OLGA *turns off the radio. She remains motionless, staring straight ahead of her. A pause. A knock at the door. She starts to her feet. Another knock. She goes slowly to the door. More rapping.*]

OLGA : Who is it?

THE VOICE OF HUGO : Hugo.

OLGA : Who?

THE VOICE OF HUGO : Hugo Barine.

[OLGA *gives a start, then remains motionless by the door.*]

THE VOICE OF HUGO : Don't you recognize my voice? Come on, open up! Let me in.

[OLGA *goes quickly to the chest of drawers, takes an object from the drawer with her left hand, covers the hand with a towel, and goes to the door. She jumps back suddenly, ready for any emergency. A tall young man, about twenty-three years old, stands in the doorway.*]

HUGO : It's me. [*They face each other silently for a moment.*] You're surprised?

OLGA : You've changed a lot.

HUGO : Yes. I've changed. [*A pause.*] You've had a good look? You recognize me? Absolutely sure? [*Pointing to the revolver hidden in the towel*] Then you can put that away.

OLGA [*still holding the revolver*] : I thought you got five years.

HUGO : Well, yes: I did get five years.

OLGA : Come in and shut the door. [*She takes a step*

backwards. The revolver is not trained directly on HUGO, *but could cover him instantly if necessary.* HUGO *looks at the revolver with some amusement and slowly turns his back to* OLGA, *then shuts the door.*] Did you escape?

HUGO: Escape? I'm not that crazy. They had to push me out bodily. [*A pause.*] I was released for good behavior.

OLGA: Are you hungry?

HUGO: You'd like me to be, wouldn't you?

OLGA: Why should I?

HUGO: It is so comforting to give; it keeps the other person at a distance. And then, when a man is eating, he seems harmless. [*A pause.*] I'm sorry: I'm neither hungry nor thirsty.

OLGA: You might just have said no.

HUGO: Don't you remember what I'm like? I talked too much.

OLGA: I remember.

HUGO [*looking the place over*]: What a desert! And yet it's all here. My typewriter?

OLGA: Sold.

HUGO: Ah! [*A pause. He looks the room over once more.*] It's empty.

OLGA: What's empty?

HUGO [*with a sweep about the room*]: This place! The furniture seems set in a desert. Back there, when I put out my arms, I could touch both walls at once. Come closer. [*She maintains her distance.*] Of course; outside of prison people live at a respectful distance. What a waste of space! It's funny to be free; it makes me dizzy. I shall have to get used all over again to speaking to people without touching them.

OLGA : When were you released?

HUGO : Just now.

OLGA : You came straight here?

HUGO : Where would you want me to go?

OLGA : You didn't talk to anyone?

[HUGO *looks at her and begins to laugh.*]

HUGO : No, Olga. No. Relax. I spoke to nobody.

[OLGA *unfreezes a bit and looks at him.*]

OLGA : They didn't shave your head.

HUGO : No.

OLGA : But they took away your wave.

[*A pause.*]

HUGO : Aren't you glad to see me?

OLGA : I'm not sure. [*A car going up the road. Motor horns, the hum of an engine.* HUGO *shudders. The automobile fades.* OLGA *watches* HUGO *coldly.*] If it's true that they let you go, you don't have to be afraid.

HUGO [*ironically*] : You think not? [*He shrugs his shoulders. A pause.*] How's Louis?

OLGA : O.K.

HUGO : And Laurent?

OLGA : He—was unlucky.

HUGO : I thought as much. Somehow or other—I don't know why—I got into the habit of thinking of him as dead. There must have been changes.

OLGA : It has become much more difficult since the Germans are here.

HUGO [*with indifference*] : That's right. They are here.

OLGA : They've been here for three months. Five divisions. Supposedly they were going on to Hungary. Then they stayed.

HUGO : Aha! [*With more interest*] There are new comrades?

OLGA : Many.

HUGO : Young ones?

OLGA : Quite a few young men. Recruiting is a little different now. There are vacancies to be filled. We are less—strict.

HUGO : Of course, of course; you have to adapt yourself. [*With a certain uneasiness*] But in all essentials the line is the same?

OLGA [*embarrassed*] : Well, yes! Roughly speaking, it's the same, naturally.

HUGO : In other words, you've kept on living. In prison it's hard to believe that others go on living. And you —is there somebody in your life?

OLGA : A few. [*In response to a gesture by* HUGO] But nobody at the moment.

HUGO : Did you—ever talk about me?

OLGA [*obviously lying*] : Sometimes.

HUGO : They came at night on their bikes, just as in my day; they'd sit around the table; Louis would be there stuffing his pipe and somebody would say: "You know, it was just on a night like this that the kid asked for his special permission."

OLGA : Something like that.

HUGO : And you would say: "The kid came through fine; he did the job cleanly and without compromising anyone."

OLGA : Yes, yes, yes.

HUGO : Sometimes the rain woke me; I'd say to myself: "They're going to have rain"; and then, before going back to sleep: "Maybe tonight they'll talk about me." That was my main advantage over the dead; I could still imagine that you were thinking of me. [OLGA *takes his arm with a sudden awkward and involuntary gesture. They look at each other.* OLGA *releases* HUGO's *arm. He stiffens a bit.*] And then one day you said to yourself: "He has still three years to serve, and when he gets out [*changing his tone without taking his eyes off* OLGA], when he gets out they'll shoot him down like a dog for his trouble."

OLGA [*hastily stepping back*] : Are you crazy?

HUGO : Come on, Olga. Come on now. [*A pause.*] It was you they had send me the chocolates?

OLGA : What chocolates?

HUGO : Come, come, now!

OLGA [*imperiously*] : What chocolates?

HUGO : The brandied chocolates, in a pink box. For six months someone named Dresch sent me packages regularly. Since I knew nobody by that name, I assumed that the packages came from you, and it made me happy. Then the shipments stopped and I said to myself: "They are forgetting about me." And then, three months ago, a package arrived from the same address, with chocolates and cigarettes. I smoked the cigarettes and my cell-mate ate the chocolates. They had a bad effect on him, poor fellow, very bad. Then I thought: "They have not forgotten me."

OLGA : So?

HUGO : That's all.

OLGA : Hœderer had friends who don't exactly love you.

HUGO : They wouldn't have waited two years to let me know how they felt. No, Olga, I've had all the time in the world to think and there's only one way of explaining it: at first the party thought I could still be used in some way, and then it changed its mind.

OLGA [*without severity*] : You talk too much, Hugo. Always have. You have to talk to make sure you're alive.

HUGO : I won't argue about that; I do talk too much. I know it only too well, and you've never trusted me. No need to go any further. [*A pause.*] I'm not holding anything against you, you know. This whole affair began badly.

OLGA : Hugo, look at me. Do you really mean what you said? [*She looks him full in the face.*] Yes, you meant it. [*Violently*] Then why did you come here? Why? Why?

HUGO : Because I knew that *you* couldn't shoot me. [*He glances at the gun that she still holds and smiles.*] At least I don't think so. [OLGA *ill-humoredly throws the revolver, still wrapped in the towel, on the table.*] You see.

OLGA : Look here, Hugo: I don't believe a word of what you have told me and I have received no instructions in regard to you. But if ever I should, you must know that I will do as I am told. And if anyone from the party asks me, I should say that you are here, even if they were to shoot you down before my eyes. Have you any money?

HUGO: No.

OLGA: I'll give you some, then you will go.

HUGO: Where? To wander around the alleys of the harbor or on the docks? The water is cold, Olga. Here, whatever happens, it is light and warm. It's a more comfortable end.

OLGA: Hugo, I shall do as the party tells me. I swear to you I shall do whatever they require of me.

HUGO: What did I tell you?

OLGA: Get out!

HUGO: No. [*Mimicking* OLGA] "I shall do as the party tells me." You'll be surprised. With the best will in the world what you can never do is exactly what the party orders. "You will go to Hœderer and put three bullets into his belly." A clear enough order, no? I went to Hœderer and left him with three bullets in his belly. But that was something else again. The orders? There was no order, not any more. Orders leave you all alone, after a certain point. The order stayed behind and I went on alone and killed alone —and I no longer even know why. I wish the party would order you to shoot me. Just to see. Only to see what happens.

OLGA: You would see. [*A pause.*] What are you going to do now?

HUGO: I don't know. I didn't make any plans. When they opened the prison gate, I thought that I would come here and I came.

OLGA: Where is Jessica?

HUGO: With her father. She wrote to me several times, in the beginning. I think she has dropped my name.

OLGA: Where could I put you up? Comrades comes here every day. They come and go as they wish.

HUGO: Into your bedroom, too?

OLGA: No.

HUGO: I used to go in there. There was a red quilt on the bed; the wallpaper was covered with yellow and green diamonds; there were two photographs, and one was of me.

OLGA: What's this? An inventory?

HUGO: No: I remember. I often thought of it. But the other photo was a problem. I couldn't remember who it was.

[*A car on the road; he gives a start. They are both silent. The auto stops. The car door is slammed. A knock.*]

OLGA: Who's there?

THE VOICE OF CHARLES: Charles.

HUGO [*softly*]: Who is Charles?

OLGA [*softly*]: One of our men.

HUGO [*looking at her*]: Now what? [*A very brief pause. Charles knocks again.*]

OLGA [*to* HUGO]: Well? What are you waiting for? Go into my room. You can finish your reminiscing. [HUGO *goes out.* OLGA *goes to open the door.* CHARLES *and* FRANTZ *enter.*]

CHARLES: Where is he?

OLGA: Who?

CHARLES: The guy. He's been tailed ever since he—

[*A brief pause.*] Isn't he here?

OLGA : Yes. He's here.

CHARLES : Where?

OLGA : There. [*She indicates her room.*]

CHARLES : Good.

[*He signals to* FRANTZ *to follow him, reaches into his coat pocket, and takes a step forward.* OLGA *bars the way.*]

OLGA : No.

CHARLES : It won't take long, Olga. If you like, you can take a walk. When you get back, there'll be nobody here and no traces. [*Indicating* FRANTZ] The kid is here to clean up afterwards.

OLGA : No.

CHARLES : Let me do my job, Olga.

OLGA : Louis sent you?

CHARLES : Yes.

OLGA : Where is he?

CHARLES : In the car.

OLGA : Go get him. [CHARLES *hesitates.*] Go on! I tell you go get him.

[CHARLES *makes a motion and* FRANTZ *goes out.* OLGA *and* CHARLES *face each other in silence.* OLGA, *without taking her eyes from his, gathers up the towel-covered revolver from the table.*]

LOUIS [*entering*] : What's got into you? Why don't you let them do their job?

OLGA : You are in too much of a hurry.

LOUIS : In too much of a hurry?

OLGA : Send them away.

LOUIS [*to the men*] : Wait for me outside. Come if I

call. [*They go out.*] So. Now what have you to tell
me? [*A pause.*]

OLGA [*gently*] : Louis, he worked for us.

LOUIS : Don't be a child, Olga. This fellow is dangerous.
He must not talk.

OLGA : He won't talk.

LOUIS : Him? That damned chatterbox—

OLGA : He won't talk.

LOUIS : I wonder if you see him as he really is. You always were kind of sweet on him.

OLGA : And you were always prejudiced against him.
[*A pause.*] Louis, I didn't send for you to discuss
our personal prejudices. I am speaking to you in the
interest of the party. We have lost many comrades
since the Germans came. We can't afford to get rid
of any young worker without even trying to find
out if he's salvageable or not.

LOUIS : Salvageable? He is an undisciplined anarchistic
individualist, an intellectual who thought only of
striking an attractive pose, a bourgeois who worked
when it pleased him and stopped at the slightest
whim.

OLGA : He is also the guy who at twenty shot down
Hœderer despite his bodyguards and managed to
disguise a political assassination as a crime of passion.

LOUIS : But was it a political assassination? That part of
the story was never cleared up.

OLGA : Exactly. We must get the true story here and
now.

LOUIS : The story stinks. I don't want to have anything

to do with it. And in any case I don't have the time
to conduct a class examination.

OLGA : I have the time. [*A gesture by* LOUIS.] Louis, I'm
afraid you are introducing too much personal feeling
into this affair.

LOUIS : And I'm afraid you are much too involved yourself.

OLGA : Have you ever known me to put my feelings
first? I'm not asking you to give him his life with no
strings attached. I don't give a damn about his life. I
just insist that before getting rid of him we ought to
be sure that the party cannot take him back.

LOUIS : The party cannot take him back; not any more.
Not now. You know that perfectly well.

OLGA : He worked under an assumed name and nobody
knew him except Laurent, who is dead, and Dresden,
who is at the front. You're afraid he'll talk? In the
right spot he won't talk. You say he is an intellectual
and an anarchist? Agreed, but he is also a desperate
man. Properly supervised, he can serve as a strong-
arm man for all sorts of jobs. He has proved that.

LOUIS : What do you suggest?

OLGA : What time is it?

LOUIS : Nine o'clock.

OLGA : Come back at midnight. I shall know by then
why he killed Hœderer, and what he is today. If I
am convinced that he can work with us, I will tell
you so through the door; you will let him sleep in
peace and give him an assignment tomorrow morning.

LOUIS : And if he isn't salvageable?

OLGA : I'll let you in.

LOUIS : A lot risked, little gained.

OLGA : Where is the risk? Are there men around the house?

LOUIS : Four.

OLGA : Let them stay there until midnight. [LOUIS *doesn't move.*] Louis, he worked for us. We must give him his chance.

LOUIS : All right. See you at midnight. [*He goes out.*] [OLGA *goes to the door and opens it.* HUGO *comes out from her room.*]

HUGO : It was your sister.

OLGA : Who?

HUGO : The picture on the wall is of your sister. [*A pause.*] My snapshot, you took it down. [OLGA *doesn't reply. He looks at her.*] You have a strange look. What did they want?

OLGA : They were looking for you.

HUGO : Ah! And you told them I was here?

OLGA : Yes.

HUGO : Very well. [*He is about to go out.*]

OLGA : The night is clear and there are comrades all around the house.

HUGO : Aha! [*He sits at the table.*] Give me something to eat. [OLGA *fetches a plate, bread, and ham. As she sets the food before him,* HUGO *chatters away.*] I had your room down pat. I was right about every detail. Everything is as it was in my memory. [*A pause.*] Only, when I was in jail, I said to myself: "This is just a memory. The real room is over there, on the other side of the wall." I went in, I looked at your

room, and it seemed no more real than my recollec-
tion. The cell, too, was a dream. And the eyes of
Hœderer, the day I shot him. Do you think there's a
chance that I'll ever wake? Perhaps when your pals
get to work on me with their playthings—

OLGA : As long as you are here they won't touch you.

HUGO : You managed that, did you? [*He pours a glass
of wine.*] I'll have to leave eventually anyhow.

OLGA : Wait. You have one night. A lot can happen in
one night.

HUGO : What do you expect to happen?

OLGA : Things can change.

HUGO : What?

OLGA : You. Me.

HUGO : You?

OLGA : That depends on you.

HUGO : So I have to change you? [*He laughs, looks at
her, gets up, and goes toward her. On the alert, she
slips quickly out of his reach.*]

OLGA : Not that way. That way I can be changed only
if I really want to be.

[*A pause.* HUGO *shrugs his shoulders and sits down
again. He begins to eat.*]

HUGO : And so?

OLGA : And so why don't you come in with us again?

HUGO [*breaking into laughter*] : You picked just the
right moment to ask me that.

OLGA : But what if it were possible? What if this whole
affair were due to a misunderstanding? Didn't you
ever think about what you would do when you got
out?

HUGO : No.

OLGA : What did you think of?

HUGO : About what I had done. I tried to understand why I did it.

OLGA : And did you come to understand? [HUGO *shrugs his shoulders.*] How did it happen? Is it true that Jessica was at the bottom of it?

HUGO : Yes.

OLGA : Then it was out of jealousy that—

HUGO : I don't know. I—don't think so.

OLGA : Tell me.

HUGO : What?

OLGA : Everything. From the beginning.

HUGO : Telling it, that's not hard; I know it by heart; I recited it to myself every day I was in prison. But what it means, that's something else again. It's an idiotic story, like all stories. If you look at it from a distance, everything holds together, more or less; but if you get up close to it, it busts apart. One action is over too quickly. It seems to happen almost spontaneously and you don't know whether you did it because you wanted to or because you couldn't hold it back. The fact is that I pulled the trigger—

OLGA : Begin at the beginning.

HUGO : You know the beginning as well as I do. Besides, does it really have a beginning? You could begin the story in March of '43 when Louis sent for me. Or a year earlier, when I joined the party. Or perhaps earlier still, with my birth. But never mind. Let's say that everything began in March 1943.

[*While he is speaking, the stage slowly darkens.*]

A C T I I

Same set. OLGA's *place, two years earlier. It is night.
Through the back door, opening on the court, comes
the hum of voices, now rising, now falling. Evidently
several persons are engaged in heated discussion.*
HUGO *is typing. He seems much more youthful than in
the previous scene.* IVAN *is pacing back and forth.*

IVAN : Hey!

HUGO : What?

IVAN : Couldn't you stop typing?

HUGO : Why?

IVAN : It gets on my nerves.

HUGO : You don't seem the nervous type.

IVAN : I'm not! But right now it bothers me. Can't you
talk to me?

HUGO [*eagerly*] : I should like nothing better. What's
your name?

IVAN : In the underground I'm known as Ivan. What's
yours?

HUGO : Raskolnikov.

IVAN [*laughing*] : What a name!

HUGO : It's my name in the party.

IVAN : Where'd you dig that up?

HUGO : It's some guy in a novel.

IVAN : What does he do?

HUGO : He kills.

IVAN : Oh. And have you killed?

HUGO : No. [*A pause.*] Who sent you here?

IVAN : Louis.

HUGO : And what are you supposed to do?

IVAN : I'm supposed to wait here until ten o'clock.

HUGO : And then what?

[*A gesture by* IVAN *indicating that* HUGO *is not to pursue this point.*]

[*Loud voices from the rear. Apparently there is some dispute.*]

IVAN : What are the boys cooking up, back there?

[*A gesture by* HUGO, *mimicking that of* IVAN *just before, indicating that* IVAN *is not to question him further.*]

HUGO : You see. That's what's such a mess; conversation can't go beyond a certain point. [*A pause.*]

IVAN : You been in the party long?

HUGO : Since 1942; that makes a year. I joined when the Regent declared war on the Soviet Union. How about you?

IVAN : I don't remember any more. I sometimes think I've always been in the party. [*A pause.*] You put out the paper, don't you?

HUGO : Myself and some others.

IVAN : I often get hold of it, but I seldom read it. It's not your fault of course, but your news is always a week behind the BBC or the Soviet radio.

HUGO : Where do you expect us to get the news? We listen to the radio just like you.

IVAN : I'm not complaining. You do your job; no offense. [*A pause.*] What time is it?

HUGO : Five minutes to ten.

IVAN : Whew! [*He yawns.*]

HUGO : What's wrong with you?

IVAN : Nothing.

HUGO : You're not feeling well.

IVAN : Sure. It's O.K.

HUGO : You're so fidgety.

IVAN : It's O.K., I tell you. I'm always like this just before.

HUGO : Before what?

IVAN : Never mind. [*A pause.*] When I'm on my bike I'll feel better. [*A pause.*] I'm too easy-going. If I didn't have to, I wouldn't hurt a fly. [*He yawns.*]
[OLGA *comes in through the front door. She sets a suitcase down by the door.*]

OLGA [*to* IVAN] : There it is. Can you tie it on your baggage-carrier?

IVAN : Let's have a look at it. Yes. Easily.

OLGA : It's ten o'clock. You can beat it now. You've been posted on the gateway and the house?

IVAN : Yes.

OLGA : Then good luck.

IVAN : None of that stuff. [*A pause.*] Are you going to kiss me?

OLGA : Sure. [*She kisses him on both cheeks.*]
[IVAN *picks up the suitcase and then, on the point of going out, turns round to face* HUGO.]

IVAN [*with comic emphasis*] : Good-by, Raskolnikov. [*He goes out.*]

HUGO [*smiling*] : Go to hell.

OLGA : You shouldn't have said that.

HUGO : Why not?

OLGA : One doesn't say things like that.

HUGO [*astonished*] : Olga, are *you* superstitious?

OLGA [*upset*] : Certainly not.

[HUGO *watches her attentively.*]

HUGO : What is he going to do?

OLGA : It's no business of yours.

HUGO : He's going to bomb the Korsk bridge?

OLGA : Why do you want me to tell you? If something goes wrong, the less you know, the better off you are.

HUGO : But *you* know, you know what he's going to do?

OLGA [*shrugging her shoulders*] : Oh, me!

HUGO : You, of course, you could keep your mouth shut. You're like Louis; you'd die before you'd talk. [*A brief silence.*] What makes you think I would talk? How will you ever be able to trust me if you don't put me to the test?

OLGA : The party isn't a night school. We're not testing your potentialities, but trying to make use of whatever capabilities you have now.

HUGO [*pointing to the typewriter*] : And my talents lie here?

OLGA : Do you know how to loosen railroad tracks?

HUGO : No.

OLGA : You see. [*A moment of silence.* HUGO *looks at himself in the mirror.*] Do you like your looks?

HUGO : I want to see if I look like my father. [*A pause.*] With a mustache the resemblance would be striking.

OLGA [*shrugging her shoulders*] : What of it?

HUGO : I don't like my father.

OLGA : We all know that.

HUGO : He said to me: "In my day I, too, belonged to a revolutionary group; I wrote for their paper. You'll get over it just as I did. . . ."

OLGA : Why are you telling me this?

HUGO : No reason. It's just that I think of it every time I look in the mirror. That's all.

OLGA [*pointing to the door behind which the meeting is being held*] : Is Louis in there?

HUGO : Yes.

OLGA : And Hœderer?

HUGO : I don't know him, but I suppose so. Just who is he?

OLGA : He was a deputy to the Landstag before it was dissolved. Now he's general secretary of the party. Hœderer is not his real name.

HUGO : What is his real name?

OLGA : I've already told you that you ask too many questions.

HUGO : What a racket! They must be squabbling.

OLGA : Hœderer called the committee here to have them vote on a proposition.

HUGO : What proposition?

OLGA : I don't know. I only know that Louis is against it.

HUGO [*smiling*] : If he's against it, then I am, too. I don't even have to know what the proposal is. [*A pause.*] Olga, you've got to help me.

OLGA : How?

HUGO : By convincing Louis that he should give me

something real to do. I'm tired of scribbling while
our comrades are dying.

OLGA : You run risks, too.

HUGO : Not the same thing. [*A pause.*] Olga, I have no
wish to live.

OLGA : Really? Why not?

HUGO [*grimacing*] : Too difficult.

OLGA : Just the same, you got married.

HUGO : Bah!

OLGA : And you love your wife.

HUGO : Yes. Of course. [*A pause.*] A man who doesn't
want to live can do many things, if you know how to
use him. [*A pause. There is an uproar in the adjoin-
ing room.*] It sounds bad in there.

OLGA [*disturbed*] : Very bad.

[LOUIS *emerges with two other men, who leave
precipitately by the front door.*]

LOUIS : It's all over.

OLGA : Hœderer?

LOUIS : He went out the back way with Boris and
Lucas.

OLGA : Well?

[LOUIS *shrugs his shoulders without replying. A
pause. Then:*]

LOUIS : The dirty bastards!

OLGA : It was put to a vote?

LOUIS : Yes. [*A pause.*] He is authorized to begin negotiations. When he returns with a definite offer,
he'll carry it through.

OLGA : When is the next meeting?

LOUIS : In ten days. That gives us more than a week.

[OLGA *points to* HUGO.] What? Oh! Yes. So you're
still here, huh? [*He looks at him and repeats absent-
mindedly*:] You're still here. [HUGO *is about to
leave.*] Stay. I may have some work for you. [*To*
OLGA] You know him better than I do. What's he
worth?

OLGA : He'll do.

LOUIS : You don't think he'd get cold feet in the middle?

OLGA : Oh no! Not that. On the contrary, he—

LOUIS : What?

OLGA : Nothing. He'll do.

LOUIS : Good. [*A pause.*] Has Ivan gone?

OLGA : A quarter of an hour ago.

LOUIS : We're sitting right up in the box seats; we
should be able to hear the explosion from here. [*A
pause. He turns again toward* HUGO.] It seems you
want to *act?*

HUGO : Yes.

LOUIS : Why?

HUGO : Just because.

LOUIS : Excellent. Only you can't do anything with
your hands.

HUGO : That's true. I don't know how to do anything.

LOUIS : Well, then?

HUGO : In Russia at the end of the last century there
were characters who would place themselves in the
path of a grand duke with bombs in their pockets.
The bombs would go off, the grand duke would get
blown up, and the guys too. That's the sort of thing I
can do.

LOUIS : They were anarchists. You think of them because you belong to the same type; you are an intellectual and an anarchist. You are fifty years behind
the times. Terrorism, that's finished.

HUGO : Then I'm good for nothing.

LOUIS : In that field, yes.

HUGO : Let's drop the subject.

LOUIS : Wait. [*A pause.*] I may be able to find something for you to do.

HUGO : *Real* work?

LOUIS : Why not?

HUGO : You'll *really* trust me?

LOUIS : That depends on you.

HUGO : Louis, I shall do whatever you want, no matter
what.

LOUIS : We shall see. Sit down. [*A pause.*] Here is the
situation: on one side there is the fascist government
of the Regent, which has lined itself up with the Axis;
on the other side there is our party, which is fighting for democracy, for liberty, for a classless society. Between these two forces there is the Pentagon,
which serves as a clandestine rallying-point for the
bourgeois liberals and nationalists. Three groups with
irreconcilable interests, three groups who hate each
other. [*A pause.*] Hœderer had us meet tonight because he wants the Proletarian Party to join forces
with the fascists and the Pentagon and share power
with them after the war. What do you think of that?

HUGO [*smiling*] : You're pulling my leg.

LOUIS : Why?

HUGO : Because it's too idiotic.

LOUIS : And yet that's just what we've been discussing here for three hours.

HUGO : It's [*confused*]—it's as if you told me that Olga had denounced us all to the police and that the party had voted to thank her for it.

LOUIS : What would you do if the majority of the party came out in favor of conciliation?

HUGO : Are you serious?

LOUIS : Yes.

HUGO : I abandoned my family and my class the day I understood what oppression was. Under no circumstances will I compromise with them.

LOUIS : But if it came down to that?

HUGO : Then I would get hold of a bomb and kill a cop in Royal Square, or with a bit of luck one of the military police. Then I would wait beside the body to see what would happen. [*A pause.*] But this is all a joke.

LOUIS : The Central Committee has accepted Hœderer's proposal, four votes to three. Next week Hœderer is to negotiate with the Regent's men.

HUGO : Has he sold out?

LOUIS : I don't know and I don't give a damn. Objectively he is a traitor; that's all that concerns me.

HUGO : But, Louis—I just don't understand; it's—it's absurd. The Regent hates us, hunts us down, makes war on the U.S.S.R. as the ally of Germany; he has had our comrades shot; how could he—?

LOUIS : The Regent no longer believes in an Axis victory; he wants to save his skin. If the Allies win, he wants to be able to say he was playing a double game.

HUGO: But our pals—

LOUIS: The whole P.A.C., which I represent, is against Hœderer. But the Proletarian Party, as you know, came into existence through the fusion of the P.A.C. and the Social Democrats. The Social Democrats have voted for Hœderer's proposal, and they are in the majority.

HUGO: But why did they—?

LOUIS: Because he scared them.

HUGO: Can't we break with them?

LOUIS: A split? Impossible. [*A pause.*] Are you with us, kid?

HUGO: Olga and you taught me all I know. I owe everything to you. To me, you are the party.

LOUIS [*to* OLGA] Does he mean what he says?

OLGA: Yes.

LOUIS: Good. [*To* HUGO] You get the situation. As things stand, we can't walk out and we can't carry the matter to the committee. But the whole thing boils down to a maneuver of Hœderer's. If it weren't for Hœderer, we could put the others in our pocket. [*A pause.*] Last Tuesday Hœderer asked the party to furnish him with a male secretary. A student. Married.

HUGO: Why does he have to be married?

LOUIS: That I don't know. Are you married?

HUGO: Yes.

LOUIS: Fine! Do you accept?

[*They measure each other for a moment.*]

HUGO [*with energy*] : Yes.

LOUIS : Excellent. You can leave tomorrow with your wife. He lives about fifteen miles from here, in a country house turned over to him by a friend, with three strong-arm men, who are there in case of a sudden attack. Your job will be just to spy on him; we'll contact you once you are installed in the house. He must not see the envoys of the Regent, or in any case he mustn't see them twice. You understand?

HUGO : Yes.

LOUIS : On the night we set, you will open the door to three comrades who will finish the job; there'll be a car on the road and you can clear out with your wife in the meantime.

HUGO : Oh, Louis!

LOUIS : What's the matter?

HUGO : So that's it? Only that, huh? That's all you think I can handle?

LOUIS : You don't agree?

HUGO : No. Not at all; I won't be a decoy. People like me have pride, you know. An intellectual anarchist can't accept any old job.

OLGA : Hugo!

HUGO : This is what I propose; no need to contact me and no spying. I'll do the job myself.

LOUIS : You?

HUGO : Me.

LOUIS : It's tough work for a beginner.

HUGO : Your three killers may run into Hœderer's bodyguard; what if they are knocked off? But if I become

his secretary and win his confidence, I would be alone
with him several hours a day.

LOUIS [*uncertain*] : I'm not—

OLGA : Louis!

LOUIS : What?

OLGA [*quietly*] : Trust him. It's a young kid after his
big chance. He'll make good.

LOUIS : You'll answer for him?

OLGA : Without reservation.

LOUIS : Fine! Now listen!

[*A muffled explosion in the distance.*]

OLGA : He did it.

LOUIS : Lights out! Hugo, open the window!

[*They turn out the lights and open the windows;
far off there is the red glow of a fire.*]

OLGA : It's burning, it's burning. A regular fire! He did
it!

[*They are all by the window.*]

HUGO : He did it. Before the end of the week you will
be here, both of you, on a night such as this, and you
will be waiting to hear from me; you'll be uneasy
and you'll speak of me. I'll mean something to you
then. You will ask yourselves: "What's he doing?"
And then there will be a ring on the phone or someone will knock on the door and you will smile just
the way you are smiling now and you will say: "He
did it."

CURTAIN

ACT III

A summerhouse. A bed, cupboards, armchairs, chairs.
Women's clothes are strewn on all the chairs; there
are open suitcases on the bed.

JESSICA is putting the place in order. She goes to the
window and looks out. Returns. Goes to a packed
suitcase in a corner (it has the initials "H. B." on it),
drags it to the front of the stage, takes another look
out the window, fetches a suit of men's clothes from
a closet, searches the pockets, brings out a key, opens
the suitcase, rummages through it hastily, goes to
look out of the window, comes back to the suitcase,
rummages in it again, finds what she has been look-
ing for while she has her back turned to the audience,
and looks once more out the window. She gives a
start, rapidly closes the suitcase, puts the key back in
the coat pocket, and hides under the mattress what-
ever it is that she has found. HUGO enters.

HUGO: It went on endlessly. Were you very bored?
JESSICA: Horribly.
HUGO: What did you do?
JESSICA: I slept.
HUGO: Well, time doesn't hang heavy when you sleep.
JESSICA: I dreamed that I was bored, and that woke me
up and I unpacked the suitcases. How does the place
look now? [*She points to the jumble of clothes on*
the bed and the chairs.]

HUGO: I don't know. Is this arrangement temporary?

JESSICA [*firmly*] : No, final.

HUGO: Very good.

JESSICA: What do you think of him?

HUGO: Who?

JESSICA: Hœderer.

HUGO: Hœderer? Like anybody else.

JESSICA: How old is he?

HUGO: Middle-aged.

JESSICA: Middle between what and what?

HUGO: Twenty and sixty.

JESSICA: Tall or short?

HUGO: Medium.

JESSICA: Any unusual features?

HUGO: A big scar, a wig, and a glass eye.

JESSICA: What a monster!

HUGO: I made it up. He's perfectly ordinary.

JESSICA: You're just showing off. The truth is you couldn't describe him to me.

HUGO: Of course I could, if I wanted to.

JESSICA: No, not even if you wanted to.

HUGO: Yes, I could.

JESSICA: No. What color are his eyes?

HUGO: Gray.

JESSICA: My poor baby, you think all eyes are gray. There are blue eyes and black eyes and green eyes and hazel-colored eyes. There are even mauve-colored eyes. What color are mine? [*She covers her eyes with her hand.*] Don't look.

HUGO: They are two silk pavilions, two Andalusian gardens, two moonfish.

JESSICA : I asked you to tell me their color.

HUGO : Blue.

JESSICA : You looked.

HUGO : No, but you told me this morning.

JESSICA : Idiot. [*She comes closer to him.*] Now think carefully, Hugo: has he a mustache?

HUGO : No. [*A pause.*] I'm sure he hasn't.

JESSICA [*sadly*] : I wish I could believe you.

HUGO [*reflects a moment, then blurts out suddenly*] : He wore a polka-dot tie.

JESSICA : Polka-dot?

HUGO : Polka-dot.

JESSICA : Go 'way with you.

HUGO : You know the kind. [*He pretends he is looping a fancy ascot.*]

JESSICA : You crawled before him, you gave in! All the while he was talking to you, you were looking at his tie. Hugo, he intimidated you!

HUGO : He did not!

JESSICA : He intimidated you!

HUGO : The fact is, he's not intimidating.

JESSICA : Then why did you look at his tie?

HUGO : In order not to intimidate him.

JESSICA : Uh-huh. But when I see him and you want to know what he looks like, you only have to ask me. What did he say to you?

HUGO : I told him that my father was vice-president of the Tosk Coke Manufacturers and that I broke with him to enter the party.

JESSICA : And what did he say to that?

HUGO : He said that was fine.

JESSICA : And then?

HUGO : I didn't conceal from him that I have my doctorate, but I made him understand that I am not an intellectual, that I am not ashamed to work as a clerk, and that my special point of honor is to require of myself the strictest discipline and obedience.

JESSICA : And what did he say to that?

HUGO : He said that was fine too.

JESSICA : And that took two hours?

HUGO : There were moments of silence.

JESSICA : You are one of those people who always repeat what you say to others and never what others say to you.

HUGO : That's because I think you are more interested in me than in the others.

JESSICA : Of course, my baby. But I have you. I don't have the others.

HUGO : Do you want Hœderer?

JESSICA : I want to have everybody.

HUGO : Hmmm. But he's vulgar.

JESSICA : How do you know if you didn't look at him?

HUGO : You have to be vulgar to wear a polka-dot tie.

JESSICA : The Greek empresses slept with barbarian generals.

HUGO : There were no empresses in Greece.

JESSICA : Then they were in Byzantium.

HUGO : In Byzantium there were barbarian generals and Greek empresses, but no one reports what they did together.

JESSICA : What else could they do? [*A brief silence.*] Did he ask you what I'm like?

HUGO : No.

JESSICA : You wouldn't have been able to tell him anything anyway: you don't know anything about me. Didn't he ask about me at all?

HUGO : No, nothing.

JESSICA : He has no manners.

HUGO : You see. Anyway, there's no use your being interested in him now.

JESSICA : Why?

HUGO : You'll keep your mouth shut?

JESSICA : I'll hold it shut with both hands.

HUGO : He's going to die.

JESSICA : Is he sick?

HUGO : No, but he's going to be assassinated—like all men in politics.

JESSICA : Ah! [*A pause.*] And you, my little pet—are you in politics?

HUGO : Certainly.

JESSICA : And what is there for the widow of a political man to do?

HUGO : She can join her husband's party and complete his work.

JESSICA : Good Lord! I would rather kill myself beside your grave.

HUGO : Nowadays that only happens in Malabar.

JESSICA : Then here is what I would do: I would track down your assassins one by one, then I would make them burn with love for me, and when they began to think that they could console my haughty, despairing grief, I would stick a knife in their hearts.

HUGO : Which would you enjoy more? Killing them or seducing them?

JESSICA : You're stupid and vulgar.

HUGO : I thought you liked vulgar men. [JESSICA *doesn't reply.*] Are we playing our little game or not?

JESSICA : This isn't playing any more. Let me unpack the suitcases.

HUGO : Go ahead!

JESSICA : The only one left to unpack is yours. Give me the key.

HUGO : I gave it to you.

JESSICA [*pointing to the suitcase she opened at the beginning of the act*] : Not to that one.

HUGO : I'll unpack that myself.

JESSICA : That's not your job, my pet.

HUGO : Since when is it yours? Do you want to play at being a housewife?

JESSICA : You're certainly playing at being a revolutionary.

HUGO : Revolutionaries don't need wives who are homemakers: they cut off their heads.

JESSICA : They prefer she-wolves with black hair, like Olga.

HUGO : Are you jealous?

JESSICA : I should like to be. I never played that game. Shall we try?

HUGO : If you like.

JESSICA : Good. Then give me the key to the suitcase.

HUGO : Never!

JESSICA : What's in this suitcase?

HUGO : A shameful secret.

JESSICA : What secret?

HUGO : I am not my father's son.

JESSICA : How happy you would be to believe that, my poor baby! But it's not possible: you look too much like him.

HUGO : That's not true, Jessica! You think I resemble him?

JESSICA : Are we playing or not?

HUGO : Playing.

JESSICA : Then open the suitcase.

HUGO : I swore not to open it.

JESSICA : It's stuffed with letters from that she-wolf! Or snapshots, perhaps? Open it!

HUGO : No.

JESSICA : Open it! Open it!

HUGO : No, no, and no.

JESSICA : Are you playing?

HUGO : Yes.

JESSICA : Then, fins: I'm not playing any more. Open the suitcase.

HUGO : No more fins! I won't open it.

JESSICA : It's all the same to me, since I know what's inside.

HUGO : What's inside?

JESSICA : These. [*She reaches under the mattress, then, with one hand behind her back, flourishes the snapshots with the other.*] There!

HUGO : Jessica!

JESSICA [*triumphant*] : I found the key in your brown

suit, and now I know who is your mistress, your princess, your empress. It's not me, and it's not the she-wolf. It's you, my pet, it's you yourself. Twelve snapshots of yourself in your suitcase.

HUGO: Give me those pictures.

JESSICA: Twelve snapshots of your wide-eyed youth. At three, at six, at eight, at ten, at twelve, at sixteen. You took them with you when your father threw you out, they go with you everywhere; how you must love yourself!

HUGO: Jessica, I'm not playing now.

JESSICA: At six you wore a starched collar, which must have scraped your tender neck, and then you had a velvet jacket with a fancy necktie. What a beautiful little man, what a well-behaved child! It's the well-behaved children, madame, that make the most formidable revolutionaries. They don't say a word, they don't hide under the table, they eat only one piece of chocolate at a time. But later on they make society pay dearly. Watch out for good boys.

[HUGO, *who had given the appearance of being resigned to her keeping the snapshots, lunges forward suddenly and grabs her.*]

HUGO: Give them back to me, you witch! Give them back to me.

JESSICA: Let go of me! [*He pushes her down on the bed.*] Look out, you're going to get us killed.

HUGO: Give them back.

JESSICA: I tell you, the gun will go off! [HUGO *gets up; she shows him the revolver she has held behind her back.*] This was in the suitcase too.

HUGO : Give it to me. [*He takes it, goes to look in his brown suit, takes out the key, goes to the suitcase, opens it, collects the snapshots, and puts them and the revolver into the suitcase. A pause.*]

JESSICA : What's that revolver doing here?

HUGO : I always have one with me.

JESSICA : That's not so. You never had one before we came here. And you never had that suitcase either. You bought them both at the same time. Why did you get a revolver?

HUGO : Do you really want to know?

JESSICA : Yes, and be serious. You have no right to keep things like this from me.

HUGO : You won't tell anybody?

JESSICA : I won't tell a soul.

HUGO : It's to kill Hœderer.

JESSICA : Don't tease me, Hugo. I tell you I'm not playing now.

HUGO [*he laughs*] : Am I playing? Or am I being serious? There's a mystery for you. Jessica, you are going to be the wife of an assassin!

JESSICA : But you could never do it, my poor little lamb; would you like me to kill him for you? I'll go offer myself to him and then—

HUGO : Thanks, and anyhow you would fail! I shall act for myself.

JESSICA : But why do you want to kill him? You don't even know the man.

HUGO : So that my wife will take me seriously. Wouldn't you take me seriously then?

JESSICA : Me? I would admire you, hide you, feed you,

and entertain you in your hide-away. And when the
neighbors turned us in I would throw myself on you
despite the police, and I would take you in my arms
crying: "I love you."

HUGO : Tell it to me now.

JESSICA : What?

HUGO : That you love me.

JESSICA : I love you.

HUGO : But mean it.

JESSICA : I love you.

HUGO : But you don't really mean it.

JESSICA : What's got into you? Are you playing?

HUGO : No, I'm not playing.

JESSICA : Then why did you ask me that? That's not
like you.

HUGO : I don't know. I need to think that you love me.
I have a right to that. Come on, say it. Say it as if you
meant it.

JESSICA : I love you. I love you. No: I love you. Oh, go
to the devil! Let's hear you say it.

HUGO : I love you.

JESSICA : You see, you don't say it any better than I.

HUGO : Jessica, you don't believe what I told you.

JESSICA : That you love me?

HUGO : That I'm going to kill Hœderer.

JESSICA : Of course I believe it.

HUGO : Try hard, Jessica. Be serious.

JESSICA : Why do I have to be serious?

HUGO : Because we can't always be playing.

JESSICA : I don't like to be serious, but I'll do the best
I can: I'll play at being serious.

HUGO : Look me in the eyes. No. Don't laugh. Listen to me: it's true about Hœderer. That's why the party sent me here.

JESSICA : I believe you. But why didn't you tell me sooner?

HUGO : Perhaps you would have refused to come here with me.

JESSICA : Why should I refuse? It's a man's job and has nothing to do with me.

HUGO : This is going to be no joke, you know. He seems to be a hard guy.

JESSICA : Oh well, we'll chloroform him and tie him across a cannon's mouth.

HUGO : Jessica! I'm serious.

JESSICA : Me too.

HUGO : You are playing at being serious. You told me so yourself.

JESSICA : No. That's what you're doing.

HUGO : You've got to believe me, I beg you.

JESSICA : I'll believe you when you believe that I'm serious.

HUGO : All right, I believe you.

JESSICA : No. You're playing at believing me.

HUGO : This can go on forever! [*A rap on the door.*] Come in! [JESSICA *gets in front of the suitcase, her back to the audience, while* HUGO *goes to open the door.*]

[SLICK *and* GEORGE *enter, smiling. They carry submachine guns and wear holsters with revolvers. A moment of silence.*]

GEORGE : It's us.

HUGO : Well?

GEORGE : We came to give you a hand.

HUGO : A hand at what?

SLICK : To unpack.

JESSICA : Thanks very much, but I don't need any help.

GEORGE [*pointing at the women's clothes strewn over the furnishings*] : All that's got to be folded.

SLICK : If the four of us pitched in, we could get it done quicker.

JESSICA : You think so?

SLICK [*picks up a slip strewn over the back of a chair and holds it up at arm's length*] : This folds in the middle, right? And then you smooth down the sides?

JESSICA : Yes! That's right. But I rather think you would be better doing heavier work.

GEORGE : Don't play with that, Slick. It'll give you ideas. Excuse him, ma'am; we haven't seen a woman for six months.

SLICK : We don't even remember how they're stacked. [*They look at her.*]

JESSICA : It's coming back to you now?

GEORGE : A little.

JESSICA : Aren't there any women in the village?

SLICK : Sure, but we never get out.

GEORGE : The other secretary went over the wall every night; result: we find him one morning with his head in a pond. Then the old man decides that the new secretary ought to be a married man so as to have the necessary right at home.

JESSICA : That was very delicate of him.

SLICK : But he's against us getting ours.

JESSICA : Really? Why?

GEORGE : He says he wants us to stay tough.

HUGO : These are Hœderer's bodyguards.

JESSICA : You know it's funny—I guessed as much.

SLICK [*indicating his submachine gun*] : On account of this?

JESSICA : Because of that, too.

GEORGE : Mustn't take us for pros. Me, I'm a plumber. We're doing a little extra stuff 'cause the party asked us.

SLICK : You're not afraid of us?

JESSICA : On the contrary; but I should like [*indicating the machine guns and revolvers*] to see you put those playthings away. Put that in a corner.

GEORGE : We can't.

SLICK : Against orders.

JESSICA : Don't you put them away when you sleep?

GEORGE : No, ma'am.

JESSICA : No?

SLICK : No.

HUGO : They're sticklers for rules. When I went to see Hœderer they kept me covered with their machine guns.

GEORGE [*laughing*] : That's us all right.

SLICK [*laughing*] : If he'd 'uv made a wrong move you'd 'uv been a widow.

[*They all laugh.*]

JESSICA : Your boss must be awfully afraid of something.

SLICK : He's not afraid, he just don't want to be killed.

JESSICA : Why should anyone kill him?

SLICK : Search me. But people want to kill him. His pals came to warn him about two weeks ago.

JESSICA : That's interesting.

SLICK : Oh, you get used to it. It's not even exciting. You gotta keep on the lookout, that's all. [*During* SLICK's *reply* GEORGE *takes a turn about the room with an air of pretended nonchalance. He goes to the open closet and comes out with* HUGO's *suit.*]

GEORGE : Hey, Slick. Get a load of this; is this guy well fixed!

SLICK : It's part of the job. You look at a secretary, see; he's taking dictation, and if his looks don't please you, you forget what you're thinking about. [GEORGE *frisks the suit while pretending to brush it.*]

GEORGE : Watch out for the closet. The walls are filthy. [*He hangs the suit in the closet and returns to stand by* SLICK. JESSICA *and* HUGO *look at each other.*]

JESSICA : Why don't you sit down?

SLICK : No, thanks.

GEORGE : Never mind.

JESSICA : We can't offer you anything to drink.

SLICK : Doesn't matter. We can't drink on the job.

HUGO : Are you on the job now?

GEORGE : We are *always* on the job.

HUGO : Ah!

SLICK : Fact is, you gotta be a damned saint to stick at it.

HUGO : But *I'm* not on the job yet. I am at home, with my wife. Let's sit down, Jessica. [*They both sit down.*]

SLICK [*going to the window*] : Fine view.

GEORGE : It's nice here.

SLICK : And quiet.

GEORGE : Did you see the bed? It's big enough for three.

SLICK : For four; young married couples snuggle up close.

GEORGE : All that space wasted while some people have to sleep on the floor.

SLICK : Shut up. I'm gonna dream about it tonight.

JESSICA : Don't you have a bed?

SLICK [*brightening up*] : George!

GEORGE [*laughing*] : Yeah.

SLICK : She's asking if we got a bed!

GEORGE [*pointing to* SLICK] : He sleeps on the rug in the office, and I sleep in the hall outside the old man's room.

JESSICA : And it's uncomfortable?

GEORGE : It would be tough on your husband; he seems like the delicate type. But we're used to that stuff. The worst of it is that we have no room ourselves. The garden isn't healthy, so we spend the day in the hall. [*He bends down and looks under the bed.*]

HUGO : What are you looking for?

GEORGE : Sometimes there are rats. [*He stands up straight.*]

HUGO : See any?

GEORGE : No.

HUGO : That's good. [*A pause.*]

JESSICA : Did you leave your boss all alone? Aren't you afraid that something might happen to him if you stay away too long?

SLICK : Leon's with him. [*Pointing to the telephone*] If there's any trouble he can always call us.

[*A pause.* HUGO *gets up, pale with exasperation.* JESSICA *stands up too.*]

HUGO : They're friendly, aren't they?

JESSICA : Delightful.

HUGO : And you see how they're built?

JESSICA : Like trucks! Well, you're going to have a trio of friends. My husband adores killers. He would have liked to be one himself.

SLICK : He's not built for it. He's built like a secretary.

HUGO : We'll get along marvelously. I shall be the brains, Jessica the eyes, you the muscles. Feel his muscles, Jessica! [*She feels them.*] Like iron. Feel them.

JESSICA : But maybe George doesn't want me to.

GEORGE [*stiffens*] : I don't care.

HUGO : You see, he's delighted. Go on, feel his muscles, Jessica, feel them. [JESSICA *feels them.*] Aren't they like iron?

JESSICA : Like steel.

HUGO : We're so intimate now, aren't we?

SLICK : If you like it that way, kid.

JESSICA : It was so nice of you to come to see us.

SLICK : The pleasure was all ours. Ain't that right, George?

GEORGE : Does us good to see you so happy.

JESSICA : You'll have something to talk about in your hallway.

SLICK : That's right. 'Cause at night we can say to each other: "They're so cozy now. He's holding his dear wife in his arms."

GEORGE : That'll be a big help to us.

HUGO [*goes to the door and opens it*] : Come back whenever you like. The place is yours. [SLICK *calmly goes to the door and shuts it.*]

SLICK : We're going. We'll go right away. There's just one little formality.

HUGO : For instance?

SLICK : We gotta search the room.

HUGO : No.

GEORGE : No?

HUGO : You're not going to search anything!

SLICK : Don't knock yourself out. We got our orders.

HUGO : Orders from whom?

SLICK : Hœderer.

HUGO : Hœderer told you to search my room?

GEORGE : Look here, bud, don't be an ass. I told you we've been warned; something's going to pop one of these days. You don't suppose we're gonna let you come in here without looking in your pockets. You could be carrying grenades or any of that stuff, though it looks to me like you couldn't hit the broad side of a barn.

HUGO : I want to know if Hœderer specifically instructed you to search my quarters.

SLICK [*to* GEORGE] : Specifically.

GEORGE : Specifically.

SLICK : No one gets in here without being frisked. That's the rule and that's all there is to it.

HUGO : And I say that you shall not search me. I'm to be the exception, and that's all there is to that.

GEORGE : Ain't you in the party?

HUGO : Yes.

GEORGE : Didn't they teach you anything? Don't you know what an assignment is?

HUGO : I know as well as you do.

SLICK : And when they give you an assignment, you know that you gotta carry it out?

HUGO : I know that.

SLICK : So?

HUGO : I respect orders, but I also respect myself. And I won't obey idiotic orders that were given expressly to make a fool of me.

SLICK : Did you hear that? Tell me, George, do you respect yourself?

GEORGE : I don't know. Do I look like I do? How about you, Slick?

SLICK : Are you crazy? You got no right to respect yourself if you're not at least a secretary.

HUGO : You stupid fools! I joined the party so that all men, secretaries or not, could have the right to respect themselves some day.

GEORGE : Make him cut it out, Slick, he's making me cry. No, kid, people join the party because they get fed up being hungry.

SLICK : So that guys like us will be able to eat some day.

GEORGE : Come on, Slick, cut the chatter. Open that one to begin with.

HUGO : You shan't touch it.

SLICK : Look, Junior, how do you plan to stop me?

HUGO : I can't fight against a steamroller, but if you just

put one finger on that bag we'll leave this place to-night and Hœderer can find himself another secre-tary.

GEORGE: Oh, you scare me! A secretary like you—I can make one any day.

HUGO: Well, search then, if you're not afraid to. Go ahead and search!

[GEORGE *scratches his head.* JESSICA, *who has re-mained very calm during the whole scene, comes to-ward them.*]

JESSICA: Why don't you telephone Hœderer?

SLICK: Hœderer?

JESSICA: He'll settle this.

[GEORGE *and* SLICK *glance at each other inquiringly.*]

GEORGE: That's an idea. [*He goes to the phone and dials it.*] Hello. Leon? Go tell the old man that our pal here doesn't want us to search him. How's that? Oh! Thanks. [*Coming back to* SLICK] He's gonna see the old man.

SLICK: All right, but I want to tell you something, George. I like Hœderer and all that, but if he makes an exception for this rich little mamma's boy, when all the rest of us were stripped to the skin, even the postman, I'll quit.

GEORGE: Same here. They'd better go along or we'll be the ones who'll quit.

SLICK: So suppose I don't respect myself, I have my pride just like anybody else.

HUGO: Suit yourself. But if Hœderer gives the order to search, in five minutes I'll be outside this house.

GEORGE: Slick!

SLICK : Yes?

GEORGE : Don't you think the gentleman has an aristocratic pan?

HUGO : Jessica!

JESSICA : Yes?

HUGO : Don't you think these gentlemen look like real bruisers?

SLICK [*goes up to him and puts a hand on his shoulder*] : Look, kid, if we really are bruisers, we're liable to bruise you good!

[*Enter* HŒDERER.]

HŒDERER : Why was I disturbed? [SLICK *takes a step backwards.*]

SLICK : He doesn't want to be searched.

HŒDERER : No?

HUGO : If you let them search me, I'll quit. That's final.

HŒDERER : Very well.

GEORGE : And if you stop us, we're the ones who are gonna quit.

HŒDERER [*to his men*] : Sit down. [*They sit down reluctantly. He takes a slip and a pair of stockings from the back of the armchair and is about to put them on the bed.*]

JESSICA : Let me. [*She takes them in her hands, rolls them into a ball, and then, without budging, throws them onto the bed.*]

HŒDERER : What's your name?

JESSICA : Jessica.

HŒDERER [*looking her over*] : I expected you to be homely.

JESSICA : Sorry to disappoint you.

HŒDERER [*still looking at her*] : Yes. It's regrettable.

JESSICA : Must I shave my head?

HŒDERER [*without taking his eyes from her*] : No. [*He steps away from her.*] Was it over you they were about to come to blows?

JESSICA : Not so far.

HŒDERER : Things must never come to that point. [*He seats himself in the armchair.*] No need to search the place.

SLICK : We—

HŒDERER : It's of no importance. We'll talk about it later. [*To* SLICK] What's going on here? What do you have against him? He's too well dressed? He talks like a book?

SLICK : Question of looks.

HŒDERER : None of that here. We check our looks outside. [*He considers them.*] Look, fellows, you've started off badly. [*To* HUGO] You are insolent because you are the weakest. [*To* SLICK *and* GEORGE] You are just ill-humored. You began by disliking him. Tomorrow you'll play tricks on him, and next week when I have to dictate a letter to him you'll come and tell me that he was fished out of a pond.

HUGO : Not if I can help it.

HŒDERER : You can't help anything. Don't get excited, boy. Things don't have to come to that point, that's all. Four men who live together have to get along if there's not to be a massacre. So will you please do me the favor of trying to understand one another?

GEORGE [*with dignity*] : Feelings can't be ordered.

HŒDERER [*forcefully*] : They can and they must be

among members of the same party when there's work to be done.

GEORGE : We're not in the same party.

HŒDERER [*to* HUGO] : Aren't you one of us?

HUGO : Of course.

HŒDERER : Well, then.

SLICK : We might belong to the same party, but we didn't get in for the same reasons.

HŒDERER : Everyone joins for the same reason.

SLICK : Let me tell you this: he joined to teach us how to respect each other.

HŒDERER : Come, come now.

GEORGE : That's what he said.

HUGO : And you—you joined just in order to be able to eat your fill. That's what you said.

HŒDERER : Is that right? Well, you are in agreement.

SLICK : How come?

HŒDERER : Slick! Didn't you tell me yourself that you were ashamed of being hungry. [*He turns toward* SLICK *and waits for a reply, but none is forthcoming.*] And how it infuriated you when you could think of nothing but your hunger? Didn't you say that a boy of twenty should have something better to do than be always thinking of his stomach?

SLICK : You didn't have to say that in front of him.

HŒDERER : Didn't you tell me that?

SLICK : What's that prove?

HŒDERER : It proves that you wanted your mouth full and a little something else besides. He calls that something else self-respect. Nothing objectionable in that. Everybody can use the words he likes.

SLICK : That's not self-respect. That makes me sick to call that self-respect. He uses words he finds in his head; he thinks with his head.

HUGO : What do you want me to think with?

SLICK : When your belly's growling, pal, it's not with your head that you think. It's true that I wanted to put a stop to that—good God, yes. Just for a moment, for a little moment, to think of something else—anything except myself. But that's not self-respect. You've never been hungry, and you've come in with us just to preach to us like the social workers who came to see my mother when she was drunk to tell her that she had no self-respect.

HUGO : That's not true.

GEORGE : Have you ever been hungry yourself? I'll bet you needed exercise before dinner to work up an appetite.

HUGO : For once you're right, my friend. I don't know what appetite is. If you could have seen the tonics they gave me as a kid; I always left half—what waste! Then they opened my mouth and told me: "One spoonful for Papa, one spoonful for Mamma, one spoonful for Aunt Anna." And they pushed the spoon down my throat. And I shot up too, believe me. But I never put on weight. Then they had me drink blood fresh from the slaughterhouse, because I was pale; after that I never touched meat. My father would say every night: "This child has no appetite." Every evening he would say: "Eat, Hugo, eat. You'll be sick." They had me take cod-liver oil; that's the height of luxury—medicine to make you hungry while others in the street would sell their souls for a beefsteak. I saw them pass under my window with their placards: "Give us bread." And then I would sit down at the table. "Eat, Hugo, eat." A spoonful for the night watchman who is on strike, a spoonful for the old woman who picks the parings out of the garbage can, a spoonful for the family of the carpenter who broke his leg. I left home. I joined the party, only to hear the same old song: "You've never been hungry, Hugo, what are you messing around here for? What can you know? You've never been hungry." Very well, then! I have never been hungry. Never! Never! Never! Now perhaps you can tell me what I can do to make you stop throwing it up to me. [*A pause.*]

HŒDERER: You heard him? Come on now, tell him. Tell him what he has to do. Slick, what do you want of him? Do you want him to cut off a hand? Or tear out one of his eyes? Or offer you his wife? What must he pay so that you will forgive him?

SLICK: I've got nothing to forgive him for.

HŒDERER: But you have. He joined the party without being driven to it by poverty.

GEORGE: We don't hold that against him. Only there's a big difference between us: him, he's just playing around. He joined up just because it was the thing to do. We did it because we couldn't do anything else.

HŒDERER: And do you think he could have done something else? The hunger of others is not so easy to bear, either.

GEORGE : There's plenty who manage to put up with it very nicely.

HŒDERER : That's because they have no imagination. The trouble with this kid here is that he has too much.

SLICK : O.K. No one's going to hurt him. We can't stand him, that's all. We have a right—

HŒDERER : What right? You have no right. None. "We can't stand him." You poor bastards, go look at your mugs in the mirror and then come back and talk about your delicate feelings if you dare. A man is judged by his work. And take care that I don't judge you by yours, because you're taking things mighty easy lately.

HUGO [*shouting*] : But don't defend me! Who asked you to defend me? You see perfectly well that there's nothing to be done about it; I'm used to it. When I saw them come in, before, I recognized their smile. Believe me, they weren't pretty; they came to pay me off for my father and for my grandfather and for all my family who had enough to eat. I tell you, I know them: they will never accept me; there are a hundred thousand of them with that smile. I struggled, I humiliated myself, I did all I could to make them forget, I told them that I loved them, that I envied them, that I admired them. Useless! There's nothing to be done about it. Nothing! I am a rich kid, an intellectual, a fellow who doesn't work with his hands. Well, let them think as they like. They're right, it's a matter of looks.

[SLICK *and* GEORGE *look at each other silently.*]

HŒDERER [*to his men*] : Well? [SLICK *and* GEORGE *shrug their shoulders uncertainly.*] I won't humor him any more than you: you know I don't humor anyone. He won't work with his hands, but I'll make him work, and hard. [*With irritation*] Well, let's get it over with.

SLICK [*making up his mind*] : O.K. [*To* HUGO] Look, buddy, it's not that I like you. It wouldn't help to try. There's something between us that just doesn't click. But I won't say that you're a bad guy, and it's true that we started off on the wrong foot. We'll try not to make life too hard. O.K.?

HUGO [*lamely*] : If you like.

SLICK : O.K., George?

GEORGE : Let it go at that. [*A pause.*]

HŒDERER [*calmly*] : Now about searching the place.

SLICK : Yes. The search. But now—

GEORGE : So all this was just talk.

SLICK : Just for the record.

HŒDERER [*changing his tone*] : Who asked your opinion? You'll search the place if I tell you to. [*To* HUGO, *in his normal tone*] I trust you, lad, but you have to be realistic. If I make an exception of you today, tomorrow they will ask me to do it again, with the result that one fine day a guy will come along and kill us all because they neglected to look in his pockets. Suppose they ask you politely, now you're friends, would you let them have a look around?

HUGO : I'm afraid—not.

HŒDERER : Ah! [*He looks at him.*] And if I were the one to ask you? [*A pause.*] I see: you have principles.

I could make this a question of principle too. But principles and I— [*A pause.*] Look at me. You have no weapons?

HUGO : No.

HŒDERER : And your wife?

HUGO : No.

HŒDERER : Good. I trust you. Get out, you two.

JESSICA : Wait. [*They come back.*] Hugo, it would be wrong not to answer trust with trust.

HUGO : What do you mean?

JESSICA : You can search anywhere you like.

HUGO : But, Jessica—

JESSICA : Well, why not? You're going to make them think you have a revolver hidden here.

HUGO : You're mad!

JESSICA : Well, then let them look. Your pride is saved, since we're doing the asking.

[GEORGE *and* SLICK *remain hesitant on the threshold.*]

HŒDERER : Well, what are you waiting for? You heard what she said?

SLICK : I thought—

HŒDERER : I don't care what you thought; do as you're told.

SLICK : O.K., O.K., O.K.

GEORGE : It wasn't worth all this fuss.

[*While they begin to search the place, slowly,* HUGO *looks at* JESSICA *with stupefaction.*]

HŒDERER [*to* SLICK *and* GEORGE] : This will teach you to trust people. I am always trustful. I trust everybody. [*They search.*] Look carefully! There's no point in doing it if you don't do it right. Slick, look in the wardrobe. Good. Take that suit out. Run through the pockets.

SLICK: Already did it.

HŒDERER: Do it again. Look under the mattress too. Good. Slick, keep it up. And you, George, come here. [*Pointing to* HUGO] Frisk him. Just look in his coat pockets. And the inside pocket. There. Now his trousers. Good. And the hip pockets. Fine.

JESSICA: What about me?

HŒDERER: If you ask for it. George. [GEORGE *doesn't budge.*] Well? You're not afraid of her?

GEORGE: Oh, O.K. [*He goes up to* JESSICA, *very red, and glides his fingertips over her.* JESSICA *laughs.*]

JESSICA: He has the touch of a lady's maid.

[SLICK *approaches the suitcase that contained the revolver.*]

SLICK: Suitcases empty?

HUGO [*taut*]: Yes. [HŒDERER *looks him over carefully.*]

HŒDERER: That one too?

HUGO: Yes. [SLICK *lifts it.*]

SLICK: No.

HUGO: Oh, no, not that one. I was going to unpack it when you came in.

HŒDERER: Open it. [SLICK *opens and rummages through it.*]

SLICK: Nothing there.

HŒDERER: Good. That's settled. You can beat it now.

SLICK [*to* HUGO]: No hard feelings.

◇◇◇

HUGO : No hard feelings.

JESSICA [*while they are going out*] : I'll come to see you in your hallway.

HŒDERER : If I were you, I wouldn't go to see them too often.

JESSICA : And why not? They're so cute, George particularly; he's like a young girl.

HŒDERER : Hmm! [*He approaches her.*] You're pretty, that's a fact. No use regretting it. Only, things being the way they are, I can see but two solutions. The first would be this: if your heart were big enough, you could make us all happy.

JESSICA : I have a very tiny heart.

HŒDERER : I thought as much. Besides, they would manage to fight just the same. The second solution: when your husband is out, you are to lock yourself in and open to nobody—not even to me.

JESSICA : Very well, but if you let me I'll choose a third course.

HŒDERER : As you will. [*He leans over her and breathes deeply.*] You smell nice. Don't use this perfume when you go to see them.

JESSICA : I'm not wearing any perfume.

HŒDERER : That makes it worse. [*He moves away from her, walks slowly to the center of the room, then stops. All the while his glance sweeps over the place. He is looking for something. From time to time his glance falls on* HUGO, *whom he watches very carefully.*] Very well. We'll let it go at that. [*A pause.*] Hugo, you're to see me tomorrow morning at ten o'clock.

HUGO : I know.

HŒDERER [*Absent-mindedly, while his eyes search around the room*] : Fine, fine, fine. Settled. Everything is fine. All's well that ends well. Yet, you look kind of funny. Everything is fine. Everybody is reconciled, we all love each other. . . . [*Suddenly*] You're fagged out, son.

HUGO : It's nothing. [HŒDERER *watches him attentively.* HUGO, *very uneasy, evidently has to make an effort to speak.*] About what happened just now—please forgive me.

HŒDERER [*without taking his eyes from him*] : I've forgotten all about it.

HUGO : In the future you'll have no cause to complain of me. I'll accept discipline.

HŒDERER : You already told me that. Are you sure you're not ill? [HUGO *doesn't reply.*] If you're sick, there's still time to tell me and I will ask the Central Committee to send someone to take your place.

HUGO : I'm not sick.

HŒDERER : Excellent. Well, I shall leave you. I suppose you want to be alone. [*He goes to the table and looks at the books on it.*] Hegel, Marx, excellent. Lorca, Eliot: never heard of them. [*He leafs through the books.*]

HUGO : They are poets.

HŒDERER [*picking up some other books*] : Poetry— poetry. A lot of poetry. Do you write poems?

HUGO : N—no.

HŒDERER : Well, you used to, eh? [*He moves away from the table, stops by the bed.*] A dressing-gown,

◇◇

you're well set up. You took it with you when you
left your father?

HUGO: Yes.

HŒDERER: The two suits also, I suppose. [*He offers
him a cigarette.*]

HUGO [*declining*]: Thanks.

HŒDERER: You don't smoke? [*A negative gesture from
HUGO.*] Good. The Central Committee gave me to
understand that you've never taken part in any direct
action. Is that true?

HUGO: Yes, it's true.

HŒDERER: That must have driven you mad. All intellectuals dream of doing something.

HUGO: I put out the paper.

HŒDERER: That's what they told me. I haven't received
a copy for two months. Were you in charge of the
earlier issues?

HUGO: Yes.

HŒDERER: You did a good job. And they deprived
themselves of such a good editor in order to send you
to me?

HUGO: They thought I was just the man you needed.

HŒDERER: They're so kind. And what about you?
Don't you object to giving up your work?

HUGO: I—

HŒDERER: The paper was made to order for you. There
were risks, responsibilities. In a certain sense that
kind of work could even be called action. [*He looks
at him.*] And now you are a secretary. [*A pause.*]
Why did you drop your other job? Why?

HUGO: I believe in discipline.

HŒDERER : Don't talk so much about discipline. I distrust people who always have that word on their lips.

HUGO : I *need* discipline.

HŒDERER : Why?

HUGO [*wearily*] : There are too many ideas in my head. I must get rid of them.

HŒDERER : What sort of ideas?

HUGO : "What am I doing here? Am I right to want what I want? Am I really just kidding myself?" Ideas like that.

HŒDERER [*slowly*] : I see. Ideas like that, eh? And at this moment your head is full of them?

HUGO [*uneasily*] : No.—No, not at this moment. [*A pause.*] But they might come back. I have to protect myself. By installing other thoughts in my head. Assignments: "Do this. Go. Stop. Say such and such." I need to obey. To obey, just like that. To eat, sleep, obey.

HŒDERER : Very good. If you are obedient we'll get along. [*He puts his hand on* HUGO's *shoulder.*] Now listen to me— [HUGO *disengages himself and steps back.* HŒDERER *regards him with increasing interest. His voice becomes harsh and cutting.*] Aha? [*A pause.*] Ha ha ha!

HUGO : I—I don't like to have anyone touch me.

HŒDERER [*in a harsh and rapid tone*] : When they searched this suitcase, you were afraid. Why?

HUGO : I wasn't afraid.

HŒDERER : Yes. You were afraid. What's in it?

HUGO : They searched and found nothing.

HŒDERER : Nothing? Well, we'll see. [*He goes to the suitcase and opens it.*] They were looking for a weapon. One can hide weapons in a suitcase, but one might also hide papers.

HUGO : Or strictly personal effects.

HŒDERER : From the moment you start to work under me, you're to understand that nothing concerning you is any longer strictly personal. [*He searches the suitcase.*] Shirts, shorts, all new. Do you have any money?

HUGO : My wife has some.

HŒDERER : What are these snapshots? [*He takes them out and looks at them. A moment of silence.*] So that was it! That was it! [*He looks at one of the snapshots.*] A velvet jacket. [*He looks at another.*] A sailor collar with a beret. What a well-dressed little man!

HUGO : Give me back those pictures.

HŒDERER : Quiet! [*He pushes him back.*] So these, then, are the strictly personal effects. You were afraid they would find them.

HUGO : If they had put their dirty paws on them, if they had so much as snickered when they saw them, I—

HŒDERER : Now we have it! The mystery is solved. That's what it is to carry your crime on your face; I would have sworn you were hiding a hand-grenade at least. [*He looks at the snapshots.*] Well, you haven't changed. These thin little legs— You sure didn't have much appetite. You were so small that they had you stand on a chair, and you crossed your arms and surveyed your world like a Napoleon. Nothing lighthearted about you. No—it mustn't be much fun to be a rich kid day in, day out. It's a bad way to begin life. Why do you lug your past around with you in that suitcase if you want to bury it? [*A vague gesture from* HUGO.] At any rate, you pay a great deal of attention to yourself.

HUGO: I am in the party to forget myself.

HŒDERER: And you think of yourself at the very moment that you should forget about yourself. Oh, well. Each one gets by the best way he can. [*He returns the snapshots.*] Hide them well. [HUGO *takes them and puts them in the inside pocket of his coat.*] Till tomorrow, Hugo.

HUGO: Till tomorrow.

HŒDERER: Good night, Jessica.

JESSICA: Good night.

[*On the threshold* HŒDERER *turns back again.*]

HŒDERER: Pull down the shades and lock the door. You never know who might be hanging around the garden. That's an order. [*He goes out.*]

[HUGO *goes to the door and turns the key twice.*]

JESSICA: He really is vulgar. But he doesn't wear a polka-dot tie.

HUGO: Where's the revolver?

JESSICA: What fun I had! This is the first time I've seen you at grips with real men.

HUGO: Jessica, where is that gun?

JESSICA: Hugo, don't you know the rules of this game:

what about the window? We can be seen from out-side. [HUGO *goes to pull down the shades and then comes back to her.*]

HUGO : Well?

JESSICA [*producing the revolver, which she has tucked inside her dress*] : Hœderer would do well to hire a woman too, when he goes frisking. I shall offer him my services.

HUGO : When did you take it?

JESSICA : When you let the two watchdogs in.

HUGO : You had the laugh on all of us. I thought he had caught you in his trap.

JESSICA : Me? I just about laughed in his face: "I trust you! I trust everybody. This will teach you to be trusting. . . ." What did he think? The trick of trusting works on men only.

HUGO : Go on!

JESSICA : Calm yourself, my darling. You were really upset.

HUGO : I? When?

JESSICA : When he said he trusted you.

HUGO : No, I wasn't upset.

JESSICA : Yes.

HUGO : No.

JESSICA : In any case, if you ever leave me with a good-looking young man, don't tell me that you trust me, because I warn you: it wouldn't prevent me from deceiving you if I had a mind to. Quite the contrary.

HUGO : I am not at all disturbed. I would leave you with my eyes shut.

JESSICA : Do you suppose that I could be touched by emotion?

HUGO : No, my little snow-woman; I believe in that coldness of snow. The most passionate seducer would freeze his fingers. He would caress you to warm you a bit, and you would melt in his hands.

JESSICA : Idiot! I'm not playing now. [*A very brief silence.*] You were really frightened?

HUGO : Just now? No. I didn't believe it was happening. I watched them search the place, and I told myself: "We're in a play." Nothing seems to me to be entirely real.

JESSICA : Not even me?

HUGO : You? [*He looks at her for a moment and then turns his head away.*] Tell me, weren't you frightened too?

JESSICA : When I saw that they were going to search me. It was touch and go. I was sure that George would scarcely touch me, but Slick would have held me tight. I wasn't afraid he would find the gun: I was afraid of his hands.

HUGO : I shouldn't have dragged you into all this.

JESSICA : On the contrary, I always dreamed of being an adventuress.

HUGO : Jessica, this isn't a game. The man is dangerous.

JESSICA : Dangerous? To whom?

HUGO : To the party.

JESSICA : To the party? I thought he was its leader.

HUGO : He is *one* of the leaders; but that's just it; he—

JESSICA : Don't explain it to me. I believe what you said.

HUGO : What do you believe?

JESSICA [*as if reciting a lesson*] : I believe that this man is dangerous, that he should be removed, and that you are going to ki—

HUGO : Quiet! [*A pause.*] Look at me. Sometimes I tell myself that you only pretend to believe in me and that you really don't, and other times I tell myself that you really believe in me but that you pretend not to. Which is true?

JESSICA [*laughing*] : There is no truth.

HUGO : What would you do if I needed your help?

JESSICA : Haven't I just helped you?

HUGO : Yes, dear, but it's not that help that I want.

JESSICA : Ingrate.

HUGO [*looking at her*] : If I could only read your thoughts—

JESSICA : Ask me.

HUGO [*shrugging his shoulders*] : What's the use! [*A pause.*] Good God, when you're going to kill a man, you should be able to feel as heavy as stone. There should be silence in my head. [*Shouting*] Silence! [*A pause.*] Did you see how big he is? How alive? [*A pause.*] It's true! It's true! It's true that I'm going to kill him: in a week he'll be stretched out dead on the ground with five holes in him. [*A pause.*] What a comedy!

JESSICA [*begins to laugh*] : My poor little darling, if you want to convince me that you're going to become a murderer, you should start by convincing yourself.

HUGO : I don't seem to be convinced, do I?

JESSICA : Not at all: you're playing your part very badly.

HUGO : But I'm not playing, Jessica.

JESSICA : Yes, you are.

HUGO : No, it's you who are playing. It's always you.

JESSICA : No, it's you. Besides, how could you kill him when I have the revolver?

HUGO : Give me that gun.

JESSICA : Not on your life: I've won it. If it hadn't been for me, you would have had it taken from you.

HUGO : Give me that gun.

JESSICA : No, I shall never give it back to you. I shall go find Hœderer and tell him: "I have come to make you happy," and when he embraces me— [HUGO, *who pretends to be resigned to letting her keep the revolver, suddenly springs on her and, as before, they fall on the bed, struggling, shouting, and laughing.* HUGO *finally seizes the gun while the curtain falls and she cries:*] Careful! Careful! It'll go off!

ACT IV

HŒDERER'S OFFICE

An austere but comfortable room. To the right, a desk; in the center, a table covered with books and papers, with a scarf that extends down to the floor. To the left, a window through which one can see the trees of the garden. To the right rear, a door; to the left of the door, a kitchen table with a gas burner. On the burner a coffee pot. Chairs of various sorts. It is afternoon.

HUGO *is alone. He approaches the desk, picks up Hœderer's penholder, and plays with it. Then he goes back to the burner, picks up the coffee pot, and looks at it, whistling.* JESSICA *enters softly.*

JESSICA : What are you doing with that coffee pot? [HUGO *hastily sets it down.*]

HUGO : Jessica, you were forbidden to enter this office.

JESSICA : What are you doing with that coffee pot?

HUGO : And what are *you* doing in here?

JESSICA : I came to see you, my love.

HUGO : Well, you've had a good look. Get out of here now. Hœderer is coming down.

JESSICA : How miserable I was without you, my little lamb!

HUGO : I have no time to play, Jessica.

JESSICA [*looking about her*] : Of course you couldn't

describe anything to me. This room smells of stale tobacco, like my father's office when I was a girl. Yet it would have been so easy to talk about odors.

HUGO: Look here—

JESSICA: Wait! [*She reaches into the pocket of her jacket.*] I came to bring you this.

HUGO: What?

JESSICA [*taking the revolver from her pocket and presenting it to* HUGO *on the palm of her hand*] : There! You forgot it.

HUGO: I didn't forget it; I never carry it.

JESSICA: Exactly: you should always have it with you.

HUGO: Jessica, since you don't seem to understand, I must tell you outright that I forbid you to set foot here. If you want to play, you have the garden and the summerhouse.

JESSICA: Hugo, you're talking to me as if I were a child of six.

HUGO: And whose fault is that? It's become unendurable; you can scarcely look at me now without laughing. It's going to be just dandy when we are fifty. We must get out of it; it's only a habit, you know, a filthy habit we formed together. Do you understand me?

JESSICA: Very well.

HUGO: Will you make an effort?

JESSICA: Yes.

HUGO: Good. Then begin by putting the gun back where you found it.

JESSICA: I can't.

HUGO: Jessica!

JESSICA: It's yours, you have to take it.

HUGO : But I tell you I have no use for it.

JESSICA : And what do you want me to do with it?

HUGO : Whatever you like, it's no concern of mine.

JESSICA : You wouldn't force your wife to go around all day with a gun in her pocket?

HUGO : Go back to our room and put it in my suitcase.

JESSICA : But I don't want to go there; you're being horrible!

HUGO : You had no business to bring it here in the first place.

JESSICA : And you shouldn't have forgotten it.

HUGO : I tell you, I didn't forget it.

JESSICA : No? Then, Hugo, you must have changed your plans.

HUGO : Be quiet.

JESSICA : Hugo, look me in the eyes. Have you changed your plans or haven't you?

HUGO : No, I haven't.

JESSICA : Yes or no, do you intend to—

HUGO : Yes! Yes! Yes! But not today.

JESSICA : Oh, Hugo, my little Hugo, why not today? I'm so bored, I've read all the novels you gave me and I don't fancy spending the whole day in bed like an odalisque; it makes me fat. What are you waiting for?

HUGO : Jessica, you're still playing.

JESSICA : You're the one who's playing. For ten days now you've put on grand airs to impress me, but he's still living. If this is a game, it's taking much too long: we have to talk in whispers all the time for fear of being heard, and I have to put up with all your whims as if you were a pregnant woman.

HUGO: You know perfectly well that this is not a game.

JESSICA [*dryly*]: Then it's much worse: I loath people who can't finish what they set out to do. If you want me to believe in you, you'll have to get it done with today.

HUGO: Today would be inopportune.

JESSICA [*in her normal voice*]: You see!

HUGO: You drive me mad! He's expecting visitors today.

JESSICA: How many?

HUGO: Two.

JESSICA: Kill them too.

HUGO: There's no one who is a worse pest than somebody who insists on playing when nobody else wants to. I'm not asking you to help me. Not at all! I simply want you not to bother me.

JESSICA: Very well, very well! Do as you like, since you insist on keeping me outside your life. But take this gun, because if I keep it it'll make my pocket sag.

HUGO: If I take it will you go?

JESSICA: Take it first.

[HUGO *takes the revolver and puts it in his pocket.*]

HUGO: Now beat it.

JESSICA: One moment! I have a right to look at the office where my husband works. [*She goes behind Hœderer's desk. Indicating the desk*] Who sits here? He or you?

HUGO [*ill-humoredly*]: He does. [*Pointing to the table*] I work at this table.

JESSICA [*without hearing him*] : Is this his handwriting? [*She takes a sheet of paper off the desk.*]

HUGO : Yes.

JESSICA [*with lively interest*] : Ha, ha, ha!

HUGO : Put that down.

JESSICA : Did you notice those flourishes? And that he prints his letters without connecting them?

HUGO : So what?

JESSICA : What do you mean, so what? It's very important.

HUGO : For whom?

JESSICA : To know his character. It's just as well to know the man you are going to kill. Look at the spaces he leaves between the words! Each letter is like a little island; the words are like archipelagoes. That certainly means something.

HUGO : What?

JESSICA : I don't know. It's so provoking: his childhood memories, the women he's had, his way of loving, all that is right there in his handwriting, and I don't know how to read it. Hugo, you must buy me a book on graphology, I feel I have a talent for it.

HUGO : I'll buy you one if you get out of here right now.

JESSICA : This looks just like a piano stool.

HUGO : That's just what it is.

JESSICA [*seating herself on the stool and spinning on it*] : What fun! When he sits down, he smokes, he talks, and spins on his piano stool.

HUGO : Yes. [JESSICA *uncorks a flask that is on the desk and sniffs it.*]

JESSICA : He drinks?

HUGO : Like a fish.

JESSICA : While he's working?

HUGO : Yes.

JESSICA : And he's never drunk?

HUGO : Never.

JESSICA : I hope that you never touch alcohol, even if he offers you a drink; you can't hold it.

HUGO : Don't big-sister me; I know perfectly well that I can't stand alcohol, nor tobacco, nor heat, nor cold, nor humidity, nor the smell of hay. I can't stand anything.

JESSICA [*slowly*] : Here he sits, he talks, he smokes, he drinks, he turns on his pedestal—

HUGO : Yes, and I, I—

JESSICA [*spying the gas burner*] : What's that doing here? Does he do his own cooking?

HUGO : Yes.

JESSICA [*bursting into laughter*] : But why? I could do it for him, since I do it for you. He could come and eat with us.

HUGO : You can't cook as well as he does; and anyway, I think he enjoys it. In the morning he makes coffee for us. Very good coffee, from the black market.

JESSICA [*pointing to the coffee pot*] : In that?

HUGO : Yes.

JESSICA : That's the coffee pot you were holding when I came in, isn't it?

HUGO : Yes.

JESSICA : What were you doing with it? What were you trying to find out?

HUGO : I don't know. [*A pause.*] It seems real when he touches it. [*He picks it up.*] Everything he touches seems real. He pours the coffee in the cups. I drink. I watch him drinking and I feel that the taste of the coffee in his mouth is real. [*A pause.*] That it's the real flavor of coffee, real warmth, the real essence that is going to vanish. Only this will be left. [*He picks up the coffee pot.*]

JESSICA : Just that?

HUGO [*taking in the whole room with a sweep of his arm*] : All that is here: lies. [*He sets down the coffee pot.*] I live in a stage set. [*He is absorbed in his thoughts.*]

JESSICA : Hugo!

HUGO [*starting*] : Yes?

JESSICA : The smell of tobacco will go when he is dead. [*Suddenly*] Don't kill him.

HUGO : Then you do believe I'm going to kill him? Answer me. Do you believe it?

JESSICA : I don't know. Everything here seems so peaceful. It all seems to remind me of my childhood. Nothing will happen! Nothing can happen, you're just teasing me.

HUGO : Here he is. Out through the window. [*He tries to force her.*]

JESSICA [*resisting*] : I should like to watch you when you are alone.

HUGO [*dragging her*] : Out, and quick.

JESSICA : At my father's place I would get under the table and watch him work for hours.

[HUGO *opens the window with his left hand.* JESSICA

frees herself and slips under the table. HŒDERER *enters.*]

HŒDERER : What are you doing under there?

JESSICA : I'm hiding.

HŒDERER : Hiding? From what?

JESSICA : I want to see what you're like when I'm not here.

HŒDERER : It's no go. [*To* HUGO] Who let her in?

HUGO : I don't know.

HŒDERER : She's your wife. Can't you control her any better than that?

JESSICA : My poor lamb, he takes you for my husband.

HŒDERER : Isn't he your husband?

JESSICA : He's my younger brother.

HŒDERER [*to* HUGO] : She doesn't respect you.

HUGO : No.

HŒDERER : Why did you marry her?

HUGO : Because she didn't respect me.

HŒDERER : When you're in the party, you marry someone from the party.

JESSICA : Why?

HŒDERER : It's simpler.

JESSICA : How do you know that I'm not a party member?

HŒDERER : That's evident. [*He looks at her.*] You're not good at anything, except love.

JESSICA : Not even at love. [*A pause.*] Do you think I ought to join the party?

HŒDERER : You can do as you please. The case is hopeless.

JESSICA : Is that my fault?

HŒDERER : How do I know? I suppose that you're half victim and half accomplice, like everybody else.

JESSICA [*with sudden violence*] : I'm no one's accomplice. Things were decided for me without asking my opinion.

HŒDERER : That's very possible. In any case, the emancipation of women doesn't interest me.

JESSICA [*indicating* HUGO] : Do you think I'm bad for him?

HŒDERER : Did you come here to ask me that?

JESSICA : Why not?

HŒDERER : I suppose you're his luxury. The sons of the bourgeoisie who come to us have a mania for bringing along with them a bit of the luxury they knew, like a souvenir. With some it's their freedom to think, with others a stickpin. With him, it's his wife.

JESSICA : Yes. And you, of course, have no need for luxury.

HŒDERER : Naturally. [*They face each other.*] Go on, now, beat it, and never set foot in here again.

JESSICA : Very well. I leave you to your masculine friendship. [*She goes out with dignity.*]

HŒDERER : You are fond of her?

HUGO : Naturally.

HŒDERER : Then forbid her to set foot in here. When I have to choose between a man and a woman, I choose the man. But you mustn't make the task too difficult for me.

HUGO : Who asks you to choose?

HŒDERER : No matter. Anyway, I chose you.

HUGO [*laughing*] : You don't know Jessica.

HŒDERER : That's very possible. And so much the better. [*A pause.*] Just the same, tell her not to come back. [*Sharply*] What time is it?

HUGO : Ten after four.

HŒDERER : They're late. [*He goes to the window, looks outside, and then turns around.*]

HUGO : Do you want me to take dictation?

HŒDERER : Not today. [HUGO *makes a move.*] No. Stay. Ten after four?

HUGO : Yes.

HŒDERER : If they don't come, they'll regret it.

HUGO : Who's coming?

HŒDERER : You'll see. People from your world. [*He paces back and forth.*] I don't like to wait. [*Approaching* HUGO] If they come, the matter is as good as settled; but if they are afraid at the last moment, we'll have to start all over again. And I believe I shan't have the time for that. How old are you?

HUGO : Twenty-one.

HŒDERER : You, you've got time.

HUGO : You're not so old either.

HŒDERER : I'm not old, but I'm on the spot. [*He shows* HUGO *the garden.*] On the other side of those walls, there are men who think night and day of getting me; and since I don't think all the time of protecting myself, sooner or later they're sure to succeed.

HUGO : How do you know they think of it night and day?

HŒDERER : Because I know them. They're always logical.

HUGO : You know who they are?

◇◇◇

HŒDERER : Yes. Did you hear the sound of a car?

HUGO : No. [*They listen.*] No.

HŒDERER : This would be the moment for one of them to jump over the wall. He'd have a chance to pull a good job.

HUGO [*slowly*] : This would be the moment—

HŒDERER [*watching him*] : You understand, it would be better for them if I were unable to receive these visitors. [*He goes to the desk and pours a drink.*] Will you have one?

HUGO : No. [*A pause.*] Are you afraid?

HŒDERER : Of what?

HUGO : Of dying.

HŒDERER : No, but I'm in a hurry. I'm always in a hurry. Once I could wait. Now I can't.

HUGO : How you must hate them!

HŒDERER : Why? In principle, I have no objection to political assassination. All parties do it.

HUGO : Give me a drink.

HŒDERER [*surprised*] : Well! [*He takes the bottle and pours a drink.* HUGO *drinks without taking his eyes from him.*] What are you looking at? Haven't you ever seen me before?

HUGO : No. I've never seen you before.

HŒDERER : For you I am only a stopping-off place. That's natural. You can look at me from the perspective of your future. You say to yourself: "I'll spend two or three years with this guy, and when he's dead I'll go somewhere else and do something else."

HUGO : I don't know if I'll ever do anything else.

HŒDERER : Twenty years from now you'll say to your

pals: "That was the time when I was Hœderer's secretary." Twenty years from now. That's rich!

HUGO : In twenty years—

HŒDERER : Well?

HUGO : It's far off.

HŒDERER : Why? Are you a lunger?

HUGO : No. Give me another drink. [HŒDERER *pours him a drink.*] I always felt I'd never make old age. I'm too much in a hurry, too.

HŒDERER : It's not the same thing.

HUGO : No. [*A pause.*] Sometimes I would cut off my hand to grow up all at once, and at other times I feel that I don't want to survive my youth.

HŒDERER : I don't know what it is.

HUGO : What?

HŒDERER : Youth, I don't know what it is: I went directly from childhood to maturity.

HUGO : Yes. It's a bourgeois malady. [*He laughs.*] And many people die of it.

HŒDERER : Would you like me to help you?

HUGO : How?

HŒDERER : You seem off to a bad start. Do you want me to help you?

HUGO [*with a start*] : Not you! [*He collects himself quickly.*] No one can help me.

HŒDERER [*going up to him*] : Look here, son. [*He stops and listens.*] Here they are. [*He goes to the window.* HUGO *follows him.*] The tall one is Karsky, the secretary of the Pentagon. The fat one is Prince Paul.

HUGO : The Regent's son?

HŒDERER : Yes. [*His expression has changed; he has an air of indifference now, hardness, and self-assurance.*] You've had enough to drink. Give me your glass. [*He empties it out the window.*] Go and sit down; listen to everything that is said, and if I give you a sign, take notes. [*He shuts the window and seats himself at his desk.*]

[KARSKY *and* PRINCE PAUL *enter, followed by* SLICK *and* GEORGE, *who cover them with their machine guns.*]

KARSKY : I'm Karsky.

HŒDERER [*without getting up*] : I recognized you.

KARSKY : You know this gentleman?

HŒDERER : Yes.

KARSKY : Then send away your watchdogs.

HŒDERER : That'll do. Beat it. [SLICK *and* GEORGE *leave.*]

KARSKY [*ironically*] : You are well protected.

HŒDERER : If I hadn't taken precautions recently, I wouldn't have the pleasure of receiving you.

KARSKY [*turning toward* HUGO] : And this one?

HŒDERER : My secretary. He's staying.

KARSKY [*going up to* HUGO] : You are Hugo Barine? [HUGO *doesn't reply.*] Are you with these people?

HUGO : Yes.

KARSKY : I saw your father last week. Would you still be interested in any news of him?

HUGO : No.

KARSKY : It is very likely that you will bear the responsibility for his death.

HUGO : It is practically certain that he bears the responsibility for my life, so we are even.

KARSKY [*without raising his voice*] : You are a little wretch.

HUGO : Tell me—

HŒDERER : Be quiet. [*To* KARSKY] : You didn't come here to insult my secretary? Please be seated. [*They sit down.*] Cognac?

KARSKY : Thank you.

THE PRINCE : Delighted. [HŒDERER *serves him.*]

KARSKY : So this is the famous Hœderer. [*He looks at him.*] The other day your men fired on ours again.

HŒDERER : Why?

KARSKY : We have a cache of arms in a garage and your men wanted them: it's as simple as that.

HŒDERER : Did they get them?

KARSKY : Yes.

HŒDERER · Nicely done.

KARSKY : There's nothing to be proud of: they outnumbered us ten to one.

HŒDERER : When the point is to win, ten to one is the right proportion. That way it's surer.

KARSKY : Let's drop the subject; I don't think we could ever come to an understanding. We just don't belong to the same race of men.

HŒDERER : We're the same race, but not the same class.

THE PRINCE : Gentlemen, let's get down to business.

HŒDERER : Good. I'm listening to you.

KARSKY : But we are the ones who want to hear from you.

HŒDERER : There must be some misunderstanding.

KARSKY : Very likely. If I hadn't thought you had a definite offer to make us, I wouldn't have troubled to come to see you.

HŒDERER : I have nothing to propose.

KARSKY : That's perfect. [*He gets to his feet.*]

THE PRINCE : Please, please, gentlemen. Sit down, Karsky. This is a bad way to begin. Shouldn't we introduce a little plain dealing into the discussion?

KARSKY [*to* THE PRINCE] : Plain dealing? Did you see his eyes when his two watchdogs shoved us in here with their machine guns? These people hate us. I consented to the interview only because of your insistence, but I'm convinced that no good will come of it.

THE PRINCE : Karsky, last year you organized two attempts against my father, yet I was willing to meet you. We haven't perhaps many reasons to like each other, but our personal feelings don't enter into it when the national interest is at stake. [*A pause.*] This interest, of course, we don't always interpret in the same way. You, Hœderer, think of it perhaps somewhat too exclusively in terms of the legitimate claims of the working class. My father and I, who have always been favorable to these claims, have been obliged, because of the threatening attitude of Germany, to relegate them to a secondary plane, because we recognized that our first duty was to safeguard the independence of our territories, even at the price of unpopular measures.

HŒDERER : You mean by declaring war on the U.S.S.R.

THE PRINCE [*continuing*] : On the other hand, Karsky and his friends, who do not share our point of view on foreign policy, have perhaps underestimated the need for Illyria to present a strong and united front to the outside world, one people behind a single leader, and they have formed an underground resistance movement. Thus it happens that men equally honest, equally devoted to their fatherland, are momentarily separated by different conceptions of their duty. [HŒDERER *laughs rudely*.] I beg your pardon?

HŒDERER : Nothing. Go on.

THE PRINCE : Fortunately today our positions are not so far apart, and it seems that each of us has a keener understanding of the point of view of the others. My father does not wish to continue this useless and costly war. Naturally we are not in a position to conclude a separate peace, but I can assure you that military operations will be conducted in the future without undue zeal. As for Karsky, he realizes now that internal divisions can only be a disservice to the cause of our country, and wants both of us to prepare for the imminent peace by bringing about a national front. Naturally this united front cannot come into the open without stirring the suspicions of the Germans, but the framework for it can be worked out in the underground organizations that already exist.

HŒDERER : And then?

THE PRINCE : Well, that's about all. Karsky and I want you to announce the good news that we agree in principle.

HŒDERER : Why should that interest me?

KARSKY : That's enough; we are wasting our time.

THE PRINCE [*continuing*] : It goes without saying that this front should be as broad as possible. If the Proletarian Party expresses a desire to join us—

HŒDERER : What do you offer?

KARSKY : Two votes for your party in the national underground committee we shall set up.

HŒDERER : Two votes out of how many?

KARSKY : Out of twelve.

HŒDERER [*pretending to be politely surprised*] : Two votes out of twelve?

KARSKY : The Regent will send four of his advisers as delegates, and six other votes will go to the Pentagon. The chairman is to be elected.

HŒDERER [*chuckling*] : Two votes out of twelve.

KARSKY : The Pentagon includes the major part of the peasantry—that is to say, fifty-seven per cent of the population—plus almost the whole of the middle class. The workers scarcely represent twenty per cent of the population, and you don't even have all of them behind you.

HŒDERER : Right. Go on.

KARSKY : We shall reorganize and fuse the structure of our two underground organizations. Your men will enter our echelons.

HŒDERER : You mean that the Pentagon will absorb our troops.

KARSKY : That's the best formula for reconciliation.

HŒDERER : How right you are: reconciliation by means of the annihilation of one of your opponents. That achieved, it's perfectly logical to grant us only two votes on the Central Committee. Even that's too many: the two votes would represent nothing.

KARSKY : No one is forcing you to accept.

THE PRINCE [*hastily*] : But if you accept, of course, the government would be ready to set aside the laws of '39 controlling the press, union organization, and labor legislation.

HŒDERER : Very tempting! [*He raps on the table.*] Excellent. Well, we have become acquainted; now let's get to work. Here are my conditions: a steering committee reduced to six members. The Proletarian Party is to have three votes; you can divide the other three as you see fit. The underground organizations are to remain distinct and separate and will undertake joint action only on the decision of the Central Committee. Take it or leave it.

KARSKY : Do you take us for fools?

HŒDERER : No one is forcing you to accept.

KARSKY [*to* THE PRINCE] : I told you that you can't deal with these people. We have two thirds of the country, money, arms, trained military groups, not to speak of the moral superiority given us by our martyrs. Here is a handful of men without a penny who calmly claim a majority of the Central Committee.

HŒDERER : Then the answer is no?

KARSKY : Definitely. We'll manage without you.

HŒDERER : Very well, then; you may leave. [KARSKY *hesitates for a moment, then makes for the door.*

THE PRINCE *doesn't budge*.] Look at the Prince, Karsky; he's sharper than you. He already understands.

THE PRINCE [*to* KARSKY, *smoothly*] : We can't reject these proposals without a discussion.

KARSKY [*violently*] : These are not proposals. These are absurd ultimatums, which I refuse to discuss. [*But he makes no move to withdraw.*]

HŒDERER : In '42 the police hunted your men and ours. You organized attempts on the life of the Regent and we sabotaged war production. When a man from the Pentagon met one of our boys, one of the two was killed on the spot. And today, suddenly, you want us all to embrace. Why?

THE PRINCE : For the good of the fatherland.

HŒDERER : Why isn't it the same good as in '42? [*A silence.*] Isn't it because the Russians beat Paulus at Stalingrad, and because the German troops are about to lose the war?

THE PRINCE : It's obvious that the general tendency of the conflict has created a new situation. But I don't see—

HŒDERER : On the contrary, I am sure that your vision is perfectly good. You want to save Illyria, of that I'm convinced. But you want to save it as it stands, with its regime of social inequality and its class privileges. When the Germans seemed on the point of victory, your father supported them. Today the tables are turned, and he seeks the favor of the Russians. But this is more difficult.

KARSKY : Hœderer, too many of our men fell in struggling against Germany for me to let you say that we compromised with the enemy to preserve our privileges.

HŒDERER : I know, Karsky: the Pentagon was anti-German. You had the perfect set-up: the Regent paid off Hitler to prevent the invasion of Illyria. But you were also anti-Russian, because the Russians were far off. "Illyria, and Illyria alone": I know the song well. You sang it for two years to the nationalist bourgeoisie. But the Russians are approaching; in a year they will be with us; Illyria won't be utterly alone. And so? You'll have to make compromises. What a stroke of luck if you could say to them: the Pentagon worked for you, and the Regent played a double game! There's just this difficulty: they don't have to believe you. What will they do, eh? What will they do? After all, we declared war on them.

THE PRINCE : My dear Hœderer, when the U.S.S.R. understands that we sincerely—

HŒDERER : When it understands that a fascist dictator and a conservative party flew sincerely to its side when its victory was assured, I doubt whether it will be very grateful. [*A pause.*] A single party has the confidence of the U.S.S.R., a single party has remained in contact with it throughout the war, a single party can send emissaries to it through the lines; only one party can guarantee your little scheme; and that is our party. When the Russians are here, they shall see through our eyes. [*A pause.*] Gentlemen, I'm afraid you'll have to do it our way.

KARSKY : I should have refused to come here.

THE PRINCE : Karsky!

KARSKY : I should have foreseen that you would reply to honest proposals with a contemptible piece of blackmail.

HŒDERER : Squeal if you like: I'm not susceptible. Squeal like a stuck pig. But remember this: when the Soviet armies are on our soil, we can take power together, your people and mine, if in the meantime we work together. But if we don't come to an understanding, at the end of the war, my party will govern *alone*. You must decide now.

KARSKY : I—

THE PRINCE [*to* KARSKY] : Violence will get us nowhere. We must take a realistic view of the situation.

KARSKY [*to* THE PRINCE] : You're a coward. You brought me into a trap to save your neck.

HŒDERER : What trap? Go if you wish to. The Prince and I can come to an agreement without you.

KARSKY [*to* THE PRINCE] : You wouldn't—

THE PRINCE : Why not? If the arrangement doesn't suit you, you don't have to accept; but my decision doesn't depend on yours.

HŒDERER : It goes without saying that my party's support of the Regent's government would put the Pentagon in a difficult situation during the last months of the war. It is also evident that we shall proceed to liquidate it completely when the Germans are defeated. But if you insist on remaining above—

KARSKY : We fought for three years for the independence of our country. Thousands of young men died for our cause. We've won the respect of the whole world. And now all of this is to go for nothing so that the pro-German party can join with the pro-Russian party and shoot us down in some dark corner.

HŒDERER: Don't be sentimental, Karsky. You've lost because you played a losing game. "Illyria, and Illyria alone"—in that slogan there's small protection for a tiny country surrounded by powerful neighbors. [*A pause.*] Do you accept my conditions?

KARSKY: I don't have the authority to accept: I'm not the only one who has to decide.

HŒDERER: I'm pressed for time, Karsky.

THE PRINCE: My dear Hœderer, perhaps we should give him time to think it over: the war isn't over and isn't likely to be in the next week.

HŒDERER: I may be finished in a week. Karsky, I trust you. I always trust people on principle. I know that you will have to consult your friends, but I also know that you can convince them. If you accept on principle today, I will speak tomorrow to my party comrades.

HUGO [*suddenly jumping to his feet*]: Hœderer!

HŒDERER: What now?

HUGO: How dare you—?

HŒDERER: Shut up.

HUGO: You have no right. They are—my God, they are the same ones! The same ones who used to come to my father's home. The same sneering and frivolous mouths, and—and they seek me out even here. You have no right, they'll slide in every place and ruin everything. They are the strongest—

◇◇

HŒDERER : Will you be quiet!

HUGO : Look here, you two: the party won't support him in this scheme! Don't count on him to white-wash you; the party isn't with him.

HŒDERER [*calmly to the two others*] : It's of no importance. A strictly personal reaction.

THE PRINCE : Yes, but this outburst annoys me. Couldn't we have your guards make the young man leave?

HŒDERER : No need for that. He'll go himself. [*He gets up and goes toward* HUGO.]

HUGO [*stepping back*] : Don't touch me. [*He puts his hand in the pocket that holds his revolver.*] Won't you listen to me? Won't you listen to me? [*At this moment a loud explosion is heard. The windowpanes are shattered, and the sashes of the window are torn off.*]

HŒDERER : Hit the ground! Duck! [*He seizes* HUGO *by the shoulders and throws him to the ground. The other two flatten out also.*]

[LEON, SLICK, GEORGE *enter on the run.*]

SLICK : You hurt?

HŒDERER [*getting up*] : No. Anyone wounded? [*To* KARSKY, *who has got to his feet*] You're bleeding!

KARSKY : It's nothing. Some splinters of glass.

GEORGE : A grenade?

HŒDERER : A grenade or a bomb. Their aim was short. Search the garden.

HUGO [*who is already by the window*] : The bastards! The dirty bastards!

[LEON *and* GEORGE *leap through the window.*]

HŒDERER [*to* THE PRINCE] : I expected something like

this. But I'm sorry that they picked this moment.

THE PRINCE : Pooh! It reminds me of my father's palace. Karsky! Are your men responsible for this?

KARSKY : Are you mad?

HŒDERER : I am the one they wanted to get. They were after me and nobody else. [*To* KARSKY] You see? It's best to take precautions. [*He looks at him.*] You're still bleeding.

[JESSICA *enters, out of breath.*]

JESSICA : Was Hœderer killed?

HŒDERER : Your husband is all right. [*To* KARSKY] Leon will take you up to my room and bandage that for you. Then we'll be able to go on with the discussion.

SLICK : You better all go up there; they might try again. You can talk while Leon patches him up.

HŒDERER : Fine.

[GEORGE *and* LEON *return through the window.*]

GEORGE : A bomb! Someone threw it from the garden and then scrammed. The wall took most of it.

HUGO : The dirty bastards.

HŒDERER : Let's go. [*He motions them toward the door.* HUGO *is about to follow them.*] Not you. [*They look at each other, then* HŒDERER *turns away and goes out.*]

HUGO [*between his teeth*] : The dirty bastards.

SLICK : What?

HUGO : The ones who threw that firecracker, they're dirty bastards. [*He goes to pour himself a drink.*]

SLICK : You're a little nervous, huh?

HUGO : Bah!

SLICK : Don't be ashamed. This is the first time, eh?
You'll get used to it.

GEORGE : I really ought to tell you, eventually it's a wel-
come distraction. Right, Slick?

SLICK : It's a change—puts you on your toes again,
takes the stiffness out of your joints.

HUGO : I'm not nervous. I'm furious. [*He takes a drink.*]

JESSICA : At whom, my little lamb?

HUGO : At the bastards who let off that blast.

SLICK : Don't let it get you down; it's a long time since
we got so excited.

GEORGE : It's our business; if it weren't for them, we
wouldn't be here.

HUGO : That's the way it is: everyone is calm, everyone
smiles, everyone is happy. He bleeds like a pig, wipes
his cheek, smiling, and says: "It's nothing." They
have guts. They're the greatest sons of bitches on
earth, and they've got guts, if only to keep you from
despising them utterly. [*Sadly*] It's a problem. [*He
drinks.*] Virtues and vices are not equitably distributed.

JESSICA : You're not a coward, my love.

HUGO : I'm not cowardly, but I'm not courageous
either. Too many nerves. I should like to go to sleep
and dream that I'm Slick. Look at him: two hundred
and twenty pounds of meat and a peanut for a brain.
He's a real whale. The peanut up above sends out
signals of fear and rage, but they're lost in all that
mass. It tickles him, that's all.

SLICK [*laughing*] : You hear that?

GEORGE [*laughing*] : He's not so wrong.

[HUGO *drinks.*]

JESSICA: Hugo!

HUGO: What?

JESSICA: Don't drink any more.

HUGO: Why not? There's nothing more for me to do. I've been relieved of my duties.

JESSICA: Hœderer relieved you of your duties?

HUGO: Hœderer? Who's talking about Hœderer? You can think what you like of Hœderer, but he's a man who trusted me. You can't say as much for everybody. [*He drinks, then goes up to* SLICK.] Some guys entrust you with a confidential mission, and you work your ass off to carry it out. And then, at the very moment you might have done it, you see that they don't give a damn for you, and that they had the job pulled off by somebody else.

JESSICA: Will you be quiet? You're not going to tell them all about our married life.

HUGO: Our married life? Ha! [*Cheering up*] Isn't she wonderful?

JESSICA: He's talking about me. For two years he's been reproaching me for not trusting him.

HUGO [*to* SLICK]: What a character, eh? [*To* JESSICA] No, you don't trust me. Or do you?

JESSICA: Certainly not at this moment.

HUGO: Nobody trusts me. There must be something wrong with my face. Tell me you love me.

JESSICA: Not in front of them.

SLICK: Don't mind us.

HUGO: She doesn't love me. She doesn't know what love is. She's an angel. A statue of salt.

SLICK : A statue of salt?

HUGO : No, I mean a statue of snow. When you caress her, she melts.

GEORGE : No kidding.

JESSICA : Come along, Hugo.

HUGO : Wait a minute, I want to give Slick some advice. I like Slick very much, I have a soft spot for him, because he's strong and never thinks. Do you want some advice, Slick?

SLICK : If I can't get out of it.

HUGO : Listen: don't marry too young.

SLICK : No danger of that.

HUGO [*beginning to show he is drunk*] : No, but listen anyway: don't marry too young. You understand what I mean? Don't marry too young. Don't take up a burden that you can't bear. Later on you'll find it's too heavy. Everything is so heavy. I don't know if you've noticed, but it's no fun being young. [*He laughs.*] A confidential mission. Well, where's the confidence?

GEORGE : What mission?

HUGO : I've been entrusted with a mission.

GEORGE : What mission?

HUGO : They would like to get me to talk, but seeing it's me, they're wasting their time. I am impenetrable. [*He looks in the mirror.*] Impenetrable! An absolute poker face. A mug like everyone else's. Anyone could see that. Good God, anyone could see that!

GEORGE : What?

HUGO : That I've been entrusted with a confidential mission.

GEORGE : Slick?

SLICK : Hmmm.

JESSICA [*calmly*] : Don't puzzle your heads: he means I'm going to have a child. He's consulting the mirror to see if he looks like the head of a family.

HUGO : By God! The head of a family. That's it. That's just what I am. The head of a family. She and I understand each other so well. Impenetrable! By which you can recognize the—head of a family. A something. A certain expression. A taste in the mouth. A thorn in the heart. [*He drinks.*] I'm sorry about Hœderer. Because, I tell you, he could have helped me. [*He laughs.*] Tell me: they're upstairs, aren't they, talking, while Leon is washing Karsky's dirty snout? What are you? Bumps on logs? Shoot me!

SLICK [*to* JESSICA] : This kid shouldn't drink.

GEORGE : He can't take it.

HUGO : Shoot me, I tell you. That's your trade. Listen closely: the head of a family is never really the head of a family. An assassin is never really an assassin. They play at it, you understand. While a dead man is really dead. To be or not to be, eh? You see what I mean. There's nothing I can be but a corpse under six feet of earth. The rest, I tell you, is clowning. [*He breaks off suddenly.*] And this too is clowning. All of it! All that I said here. Maybe you think that I'm desperate? Not at all: I'm acting out the comedy of despair. Will it ever end?

JESSICA : Do you want to go to our room?

HUGO : Wait. No. I don't know. How can I tell whether I want to or I don't want to?

◇◇

JESSICA [*filling his glass*] : Then drink.

HUGO : Good. [*He drinks.*]

SLICK : You're crazy to give him any more to drink.

JESSICA : It's just to get this over with. Now all we have to do is wait.

[HUGO *empties the glass.* JESSICA *fills it again.*]

HUGO [*drunk*] : What did I say to you? I talked about assassins? Jessica and I know what that means. The truth is that there's too much talk in here. [*He taps his forehead.*] I would like it to be quiet. [*To* SLICK] It must be so nice inside your head: not a sound, just darkness. Why do you spin around so? Don't laugh; I know I'm drunk, I know I'm ridiculous. I'll tell you: I wouldn't want to be in my own shoes. Oh no. That's not a good spot. Hold still! The whole point is too light the fuse. It seems little enough, but I wouldn't want you to have to do it. The fuse, that's what it comes down to. Light the fuse. Then everybody is blown up and I along with them: no need for an alibi. Silence. Night. Unless the dead too play comedies. What if we die and discover that the dead are alive and are simply playing at being dead? We'll see. We'll see. The thing is to light the fuse. That's the psychological moment. [*He laughs.*] But don't turn so, good God, or I'll start spinning around too. [*He tries to spin around and falls across a chair.*] Such are the benefits of a bourgeois education. [*His head droops.* JESSICA *stands over him and looks at him.*]

JESSICA : Good. It's finished. Will you help me carry him to bed?

[SLICK *looks at him and scratches his head.*]

SLICK : He talks too much, your husband.

JESSICA [*laughing*] : You don't know him. Nothing he says really means anything.

[SLICK *and* GEORGE *lift him off the chair.*]

CURTAIN

ACT V

IN THE SUMMER HOUSE

HUGO *is stretched out on the bed, fully dressed, but under a cover. He is sleeping. He tosses and groans in his sleep.* JESSICA *sits motionless at the bedside. He continues to groan; she gets up and goes into the bathroom. There is the sound of water being drawn.* OLGA *is hiding behind the window curtains. She parts the curtains and looks into the room. She makes a quick decision and approaches* HUGO. *She looks him over.* HUGO *groans.* OLGA *smooths his forehead and arranges his pillow. In the meantime* JESSICA *returns and observes this scene.* JESSICA *is holding a wet compress.*

JESSICA : How touching! How do you do, madame?

OLGA : Don't scream. I am—

JESSICA : I have no intention of screaming. But please sit down. I have more of a mind to laugh.

OLGA : I am Olga Lorame.

JESSICA : I thought as much.

OLGA : Hugo told you about me?

JESSICA : Yes.

OLGA : Is he wounded?

JESSICA : No, he's drunk. [*Walking in front of* OLGA] Allow me. [*She puts the compress on* HUGO's *forehead.*]

OLGA : Not like that. [*She rearranges the compress.*]

JESSICA : Excuse me.

OLGA : And Hœderer?

JESSICA : Hœderer? Do sit down please. [OLGA *sits down.*] It was you, madame, who threw the bomb?

OLGA : Yes.

JESSICA : No one dead; better luck next time. How did you get in here?

OLGA : By the door. You left it open while you were gone. You should never leave doors open.

JESSICA [*pointing to* HUGO] : You knew that he was in the office?

OLGA : No.

JESSICA : But you knew that he might be there?

OLGA : The risk had to be taken.

JESSICA : With a bit of luck, you would have killed him.

OLGA : That's the best thing that could have happened to him.

JESSICA : Really?

OLGA : The party doesn't like traitors.

JESSICA : Hugo is no traitor.

OLGA : I believe it, but I can't make the others believe it. [*A pause.*] This business is taking much too long: the job should have been finished a week ago.

JESSICA : You have to wait for the right moment.

OLGA : You have to *make* the right moment.

JESSICA : Did the party send you?

OLGA : The party doesn't know I'm here. I came on my own account.

JESSICA : I see. You put a bomb in your handbag and

kindly came to throw it at Hugo to save his reputation.

OLGA: If I had succeeded, they would have thought that he had given his life to kill Hœderer.

JESSICA: Yes, but he would be dead.

OLGA: However he goes about it, he hasn't much chance of getting out of it now.

JESSICA: Good friend, you are!

OLGA: Surely my friendship is better than your love. [*They face each other.*] You are the one who prevented him from doing his work?

JESSICA: I didn't hinder him in the least.

OLGA: But you didn't help him either.

JESSICA: Why should I have helped him? Did he consult me before he entered the party? And when he decided he had nothing better to do with his life than to go and assassinate a man he didn't know, did he consult me then?

OLGA: Why should he have consulted you? Could you have advised him?

JESSICA: Evidently not.

OLGA: He chose this party; he requested this mission. That ought to have been enough for you.

JESSICA: It's not enough for me.

[HUGO *groans.*]

OLGA: He's in bad shape. You shouldn't have let him drink.

JESSICA: He would be in even worse shape if he had a sliver of your bomb in his face. [*A pause.*] What a shame he didn't marry you! He needs a resolute woman. He could have stayed in your room ironing your underwear while you went out throwing bombs in the square. Then we should all have been very happy. [*She looks her over.*] I thought you were big and bony.

OLGA : With a mustache?

JESSICA : Not with a mustache, but with a wart under your nose. He always had such an air of importance when he came from seeing you. He would say: "We talked politics."

OLGA : Naturally he never talked about politics with you.

JESSICA : You may be sure he didn't marry me for that. [*A pause.*] You're in love with him, aren't you?

OLGA : What's love got to do with this? You read too many novels.

JESSICA : You've got to do something when you're not in politics.

OLGA : Set your mind at rest; love doesn't much bother women of resolution. We don't live by it.

JESSICA : Whereas I, I suppose, do?

OLGA : Like all emotional women.

JESSICA : The emotional woman is all right with me. I like my heart better than your head.

OLGA : Poor Hugo!

JESSICA : Yes. Poor Hugo! How you must detest me, madame!

OLGA : I? I haven't the time to lose. [*A pause.*] Wake him up. I have to talk to him.

JESSICA [*goes to the bed and shakes* HUGO]: Hugo! Hugo! You have a visitor.

HUGO : What? [*He sits upright.*] Olga! Olga, you

came! I'm so glad to see you; you have to help me.
[*He sits on the edge of the bed.*] Good God, what
a headache! What are we? I'm really glad to see you,
you know. Wait: something just struck me—a big
annoyance. No, I guess you can't help me any more.
As things stand, you can't help me any more. You
threw the bomb, didn't you?

OLGA : Yes.

HUGO : Why didn't you trust me?

OLGA : Hugo, in a quarter of an hour someone will
throw a rope over the wall and I'll have to go. I'm in a
hurry and you've got to listen.

HUGO : Why didn't you trust me?

OLGA : Jessica, give me that glass and that carafe.

[JESSICA *hands them to her. She fills the glass and
throws the water in* HUGO's *face.*]

HUGO : Phew!

OLGA : Are you listening?

HUGO : Yes. [*He wipes his face.*] What a headache!
Is there some more water in the carafe?

JESSICA : Yes.

HUGO : Pour me a drink, will you? [*She hands him the
glass and he drinks.*] What do the comrades think?

OLGA : They think you're a traitor.

HUGO : That's pretty strong.

OLGA : You haven't a day to lose. The matter must be
closed before tomorrow night.

HUGO : You shouldn't have thrown the bomb.

OLGA : Hugo, you wanted to take on a difficult task and
to take it on alone. I was the first to have confidence
in you when there were a hundred reasons to refuse,

and I passed my confidence on to the others. But we're not Boy Scouts, and the party was not meant to furnish you with occasions to play the hero. There's work to do and it has to be done; no matter who does it. If in twenty-four hours you haven't finished your job, we'll get someone else to do it instead.

HUGO: If I am replaced I'll leave the party.

OLGA: What kind of talk is that? Do you imagine that you can *leave* the party? We are at war, Hugo, and the comrades aren't fooling. One only leaves the party feet first.

HUGO: I'm not afraid to die.

OLGA: It's nothing at all to die. But to die so stupidly after fouling everything up; to be kicked around like a sucker; worse yet, to be disposed of like a little imbecile got rid of for fear he'll spoil everything— is that what you want? Was that what you wanted the first time you came to see me, when you seemed so happy and so proud? Why don't you say something to him! If you love him a little you can't want to have him shot like a dog.

JESSICA: You know perfectly well, Miss Lorame, that I don't understand politics.

OLGA: What have you decided?

HUGO: You shouldn't have thrown the bomb.

OLGA: What is your decision?

HUGO: You'll know tomorrow.

OLGA: Very well. Good-by, Hugo.

HUGO: Good-by, Olga.

JESSICA: See you again, madame.

◇◇

OLGA: Turn off the lights. I mustn't be seen going out. [JESSICA *turns off the lights.* OLGA *opens the door and goes out.*]

JESSICA: Should I turn on the lights again?

HUGO: Wait. She may have to come back.
[*They wait in the dark.*]

JESSICA: We could peek out of the windows and see what's happening.

HUGO: No. [*A silence.*]

JESSICA: You feel sick? [HUGO *doesn't answer.*] Answer while it's dark.

HUGO: I have a headache, that's all. [*A pause.*] Trust isn't so much, when it can't wait a week.

JESSICA: No, not much.

HUGO: How can you want to live when nobody believes in you?

JESSICA: Nobody ever believed in me, you least of all. Just the same, I got along.

HUGO: She was the only one who had a little trust in me.

JESSICA: Hugo—

HUGO: The only one, you know perfectly well. [*A pause.*] She must be safe now. I think we can put on the lights. [*He switches on the lights.* JESSICA *turns away abruptly.*] What's wrong?

JESSICA: It upsets me to see you again in the light.

HUGO: Do you want me to turn it off?

JESSICA: No. [*She turns toward him.*] You. You're going to kill a man.

HUGO: Do I know what I'm going to do?

JESSICA: Show me the revolver.

HUGO : Why?

JESSICA : I want to see how it works.

HUGO : You had it with you all afternoon.

JESSICA : It was just a toy then.

HUGO [*handing it to her*] : Careful.

JESSICA : Yes. [*She looks at it.*] It's funny.

HUGO : What's funny?

JESSICA : At this point it frightens me. Take it back. [*A pause.*] You are going to kill a man. [HUGO *begins to laugh.*] Why are you laughing?

HUGO : You believe that now! You decided to believe it?

JESSICA : Yes.

HUGO : You certainly picked the right moment; nobody else believes it now. [*A pause.*] Last week it might have helped me—

JESSICA : It's not my fault: I only believe what I see. Just this morning I couldn't even imagine him dead. [*A pause.*] I went into the office just now, and there was that fellow bleeding and you were all dead. Hœderer was dead; I saw it on his face! If you don't kill him they'll send someone else.

HUGO : I'll do it. [*A pause.*] The guy who was bleeding, that was messy, wasn't it?

JESSICA : Yes, it was messy.

HUGO : Hœderer will bleed too.

JESSICA : Be quiet.

HUGO : He'll be stretched out on the ground with an idiotic expression and he'll bleed into his clothes.

JESSICA [*slowly and in an undertone*] : Will you be quiet?

◇◇

HUGO : She threw a bomb over the wall. Certainly nothing to be proud of; she didn't even see us. Anybody can kill who isn't forced to see what he's doing. I was going to shoot him. I was in the office, I looked them in the eye and I was going to shoot. She's the one who made me miss my chance.

JESSICA : You were really going to shoot him?

HUGO : I had my hand in my pocket and my finger on the trigger.

JESSICA : And you were going to fire! Are you sure you would have fired?

HUGO : I—I was lucky enough to be mad. Of course I was going to shoot. Now we have to start from scratch. [*He laughs.*] You heard her; they say I'm a traitor. They've got it easy. Up there, when they decide that a man's to die, it's as if they scratched a name off a list; it's neat, and elegant. Here death is a chore. The slaughterhouses are here. [*A pause.*] He drinks, he smokes, he speaks to me of the party, he makes plans, and I—I think only of the corpse he is going to be; it's obscene. Did you notice his eyes?

JESSICA : Yes.

HUGO : You noticed how hard and brilliant his eyes are? And how alive?

JESSICA : Yes.

HUGO : Maybe I'll hit him in the eyes when I shoot. You aim at the belly, you know, but the gun jerks upward.

JESSICA : I like his eyes.

HUGO [*abruptly*] : It's so abstract.

JESSICA : What?

HUGO : A murder. I say, it's so abstract. You pull the trigger and after that you no longer know what goes on. [*A pause.*] If only you could shoot with your head turned away. [*A pause.*] I wonder why I'm saying all this to you.

JESSICA : So do I.

HUGO : Forgive me. [*A pause.*] And yet, if I were lying in this bed, about to die, you wouldn't abandon me, would you?

JESSICA : No.

HUGO : It's the same thing—killing and dying; it's just the same: you're just as alone. Now he has luck, he'll die only once. But I have had to kill him every minute for ten days. [*Abruptly*] What would you do, Jessica?

JESSICA : What do you mean?

HUGO : Look here, if I haven't killed him by tomorrow, I'll either have to disappear or go to them and say: do with me what you will. If I kill [*He covers his face with his hand for a moment.*] What ought I to do? What would you do?

JESSICA : Me? You're asking me what I would do in your place?

HUGO : Whom do you want me to ask? I have no one but you in all the world.

JESSICA [*slowly*] : That's true. You have only me. No one but me. Poor Hugo. [*A pause.*] I would go to Hœderer and say to him: "It's like this. I was sent here to kill you, but I've changed my mind and I want to work with you."

HUGO : Poor Jessica!

JESSICA : Couldn't you do that?

HUGO : That's exactly what's called treason.

JESSICA [*sadly*] : You see? I can't advise you. [*A pause.*] But why couldn't you do it? Because he doesn't think like you?

HUGO : If you like. Because he doesn't think like me.

JESSICA : And you have to kill the people who don't think your way?

HUGO : Sometimes.

JESSICA : But why did you choose the ideas of Louis and Olga?

HUGO : Because their ideas are correct.

JESSICA : But, Hugo, suppose you had met Hœderer last year, instead of Louis. It's his ideas that would have seemed to you to be the right ones.

HUGO : You're crazy.

JESSICA : Why?

HUGO : To hear you, one would think that all opinions have the same weight, that one catches them like a disease.

JESSICA : I didn't mean that; I—I don't know what I mean. Hugo, he is so strong that he just has to open his mouth and you're sure that he's right. And then, it seemed to me he was sincere when he said that he wanted the good of the party.

HUGO : I don't care what he thinks or what he wants. What counts is what he does.

JESSICA : But—

HUGO : *Objectively*, he's acting like a class traitor.

JESSICA [*not understanding*] : Objectively?

HUGO : Yes.

JESSICA : Ah! [*A pause.*] And he, if he knew what you are up to, wouldn't he consider you a class traitor?

HUGO : I have no idea.

JESSICA : But isn't that what he would think?

HUGO : What of it? Yes, probably.

JESSICA : But who is right?

HUGO : I'm right.

JESSICA : How do you know?

HUGO : Politics is a science. You can demonstrate that you are right and that others are wrong.

JESSICA : So in this case why do you hesitate?

HUGO : That would take too long to explain.

JESSICA : We have all night.

HUGO : It would take months and years.

JESSICA : Oh. [*She goes to the books on the table.*] Is it all written in here?

HUGO : In a way, yes. If you know how to read them.

JESSICA : Good Lord! [*She takes one up, opens it, looks at it fascinated, and sets it down sighing.*] Good heavens!

HUGO : Now let me be. Sleep or do whatever you like.

JESSICA : What's wrong? What have I said?

HUGO : Nothing. You didn't say anything. I'm the guilty party: it was mad to ask your help. Your advice comes from another world.

JESSICA : Whose fault is that? Why was I never taught anything? Why didn't you explain anything to me? You heard what he said: that I was your luxury. For nineteen years now I've been in your man's world, with signs everywhere saying: "Do not touch," made to believe that everything was going very well, that there was nothing for me to do except to arrange flowers in vases. Why did you lie to me? Why did you leave me in ignorance if it was only to confess to me one fine day that the world is falling to pieces and that you're not up to your responsibilities, forcing me to choose between a suicide and an assassination. I don't want to choose: I don't want you to get yourself killed, and I don't want you to kill him. Why have you thrust the burden on my shoulders? I don't understand this whole business and I wash my hands of it. I am neither an oppressor nor a class traitor nor a revolutionary. I've done nothing. I am innocent of everything.

HUGO : I won't ask you anything any more, Jessica.

JESSICA : It's too late, Hugo; you've got me into it, and now I have to choose. For both of us: it's my life that I'm choosing with yours, and I— Oh, my God! I can't.

HUGO : Now you understand.

[*A pause.* HUGO *sits on the bed and stares into space.* JESSICA *sits near him and puts her arms around his neck.*]

JESSICA : Don't say a word. Don't bother about me. I won't speak to you; I won't disturb your thinking. But I'll be here. It'll be cold in the morning: you'll be glad to have a little of my warmth, since I have nothing else to give you. Your head still hurts?

HUGO : Yes.

JESSICA : Here, rest it on my shoulder. Your forehead is burning up. [*She caresses his hair.*] Poor head.

HUGO [*suddenly straightening up*] : That's enough!

JESSICA [*tenderly*] : Hugo.

HUGO : You're playing mother.

JESSICA : I'm not playing, I'll never pretend any more.

HUGO : Your body is cold and you have no warmth to give me. It's not difficult to lean over a man with a maternal air and run your hand through his hair. Any girl in her teens would like to be in your place. But when I took you in my arms and asked you to be my wife, you weren't up to it.

JESSICA : Be quiet.

HUGO : Why should I be quiet? Don't you know that our love was just a game?

JESSICA : What counts tonight is not our love; it's what you must do tomorrow.

HUGO : Everything makes sense. If I had been certain— [*Abruptly*] Jessica, look at me. Can you tell me that you love me? [*He looks at her. Silence.*] There you are. I shan't even have had that.

JESSICA : And you, Hugo? Do you believe you loved me? [*He doesn't answer.*] So you see how it is. [*A pause. Abruptly*] Why don't you try to convince him?

HUGO : To convince him? Who? Hœderer?

JESSICA : Since he's wrong, you ought to be able to prove it to him.

HUGO : What an idea! He's too shrewd.

JESSICA : Why do you keep maintaining your ideas are right if you can't prove them? Hugo, it would be so wonderful if you could reconcile everybody. Everyone would be happy; you could all work together.

Try, Hugo, I beg you. Try at least once before you kill him.

[*A knock on the door.* HUGO *gets to his feet, his eyes shining.*]

HUGO : It's Olga; she's come back. I was sure she'd come back. Turn off the light and open the door.

JESSICA : How you need her! [*She goes to turn off the light and opens the door.* HŒDERER *enters.* HUGO *turns on the light again when the door is shut.* JESSICA, *recognizing* HŒDERER] You!

HŒDERER : I frightened you?

JESSICA : I'm nervous tonight. That bomb—

HŒDERER : Yes, of course. Do you usually sit in the dark?

JESSICA : I had to. My eyes are very tired.

HŒDERER : Oh! [*A pause.*] May I sit down a minute? [*He sits in the easy chair.*] Don't bother about me.

HUGO : You have something to tell me?

HŒDERER : No, nothing. You made me laugh awhile ago: you were red with anger.

HUGO : I—

HŒDERER : Don't apologize; I anticipated that. I think I would have been disturbed if you hadn't protested. There are many things I must explain to you. But tomorrow. Tomorrow we'll both say what's on our minds. But now your day is over. Mine too. A funny day, eh? Why don't you hang up some prints on the walls? That would make the place less bare. There are some in the attic. Slick will get them for you.

JESSICA : What are they like?

HŒDERER : All sorts. You can take your pick.

JESSICA : That's very nice of you. But I don't like prints.

HŒDERER : As you wish. You don't have anything to drink?

JESSICA : Nothing. I'm sorry.

HŒDERER : Too bad, too bad! What were you doing just before I came?

JESSICA : We were talking.

HŒDERER : Very well. Go on and talk. Talk! Don't bother about me. [*He fills his pipe and lights it. A very heavy silence. He smiles.*] Yes, evidently.

JESSICA : It's not very easy to pretend that you're not here.

HŒDERER : You can put me out. [*To* HUGO] You don't have to receive your boss when he has little whims. [*A pause.*] I don't know why I came. I couldn't sleep. I tried to work. [*Shrugging his shoulders*] You can't be working all the time.

JESSICA : No.

HŒDERER : We'll wind up this affair.

HUGO [*interested*] : What affair?

HŒDERER : This business with Karsky. He wants to be coaxed, but it'll go through quicker than I thought.

HUGO [*violently*] : You—

HŒDERER : Sh, sh! Tomorrow! [*A pause.*] When some business like this is about to be concluded, you feel lost. You had your lights on just a moment ago?

JESSICA : Yes.

HŒDERER : I was at the window. In the dark, so as not to be a target. You saw how calm and overcast the night is? The light slipped between the shutters of your blinds. [*A pause.*] We were close to death.

JESSICA : Yes.

HŒDERER [*with a chuckle*] : Very close. [*A pause.*] I left my room very softly. Slick was sleeping in the corridor. George was sleeping in the office. Leon was sleeping in the foyer. I wanted to wake them, and then— Bah! [*A pause.*] Then I came here. [*To* JESSICA] What's wrong? You seemed less frightened this afternoon.

JESSICA : It's because of the way you act.

HŒDERER : What do you mean?

JESSICA : I thought you didn't need anyone.

HŒDERER : I don't need anyone. [*A pause.*] Slick told me you were pregnant.

JESSICA [*sharply*] : It's not true.

HUGO : See here, Jessica, if you told Slick so, why hide it from Hœderer?

JESSICA : I was kidding Slick.

HŒDERER [*looks at her for a long time*] : Good. [*A pause.*] When I was deputy to the Landstag, I lived with a mechanic. In the evening I used to smoke my pipe in their dining-room. They had a radio, the children were playing. [*A pause.*] I think I'll go to bed. It was a mirage.

JESSICA : What was a mirage?

HŒDERER [*with a gesture*] : All that. You, too. A man must work, that's all he can do. You'll telephone the village and get the carpenter to come and repair the office window. [*He looks at him.*] You look fagged out. It seems you got drunk. Sleep tonight. You don't have to come before nine o'clock. [*He gets up.*

HUGO *takes a step forward.* JESSICA *throws herself between them.*]

JESSICA: Hugo, now is the time.

HUGO: What's that?

JESSICA: You promised me you would try to convince him.

HŒDERER: To convince me?

HUGO: Be quiet. [*He tries to disengage himself. She gets in front of him.*]

JESSICA: He doesn't agree with you.

HŒDERER [*amused*]: I noticed that.

JESSICA: He would like to explain.

HŒDERER: Tomorrow! Tomorrow!

JESSICA: Tomorrow will be too late.

HŒDERER: Why?

JESSICA [*remaining in front of* HUGO]: He—he says he doesn't want to be your secretary if you don't hear him out. Neither of you is sleepy and you have the whole night before you and—and you both had a narrow escape; that should make you feel closer.

HUGO: Drop it, I tell you.

JESSICA: Hugo, you promised me! [*To* HŒDERER] He says you are a class traitor.

HŒDERER: A class traitor! No less?

JESSICA: Objectively. He said objectively.

HŒDERER [*changing his tone and expression*]: All right. Well then, my boy, tell me what's on your mind, since we can't prevent it. I suppose I have to settle this matter before going to bed. Why am I a class traitor?

HUGO : Because you have no right to involve the party in your schemes.

HŒDERER : Why not?

HUGO : It's a revolutionary organization and you are going to make it a government party.

HŒDERER : Revolutionary parties are organized to take power.

HUGO : To take it. Yes. To seize power, arms in hand. Not to get it through some swindle.

HŒDERER : Is it the lack of bloodshed you regret? Too bad, but you ought to know that we can't get power through an armed struggle. In case of a civil war the Pentagon has the arms and the military leaders. It would serve as a perfect framework for counter-revolutionary troops.

HUGO : Who's talking about civil war? Hœderer, I don't understand you; all we need is a little patience. You yourself said that the Red Army will chase out the Regent and we'll have power alone.

HŒDERER : And what will we do to keep it? [*A pause.*] When the Red Army has crossed our frontiers, I can promise you some nasty moments.

HUGO : The Red Army—

HŒDERER : Yes, yes, I know. I too await its coming. And impatiently. But let me tell you this: all armies at war, whether they come as liberators or not, are alike. They live off the occupied country. Our peasants will detest the Russians, that's sure. How do you suppose they will feel about us, since the Russians will have forced us on them? They'll call us the party of foreigners and maybe worse. The Pentagon will go underground again; it won't have to change its slogans.

HUGO: The Pentagon, I—

HŒDERER: And besides, there's something else: the country is ruined; it may even serve as a battlefield. Any government that succeeds the Regent's will have to take terrible measures, which will make it hated. The morning after the Red Army's departure we would be swept out by an insurrection.

HUGO: An insurrection can be put down. We shall hold the country in an iron grip.

HŒDERER: An iron grip? Who will support us? Even after the revolution the proletariat will be the weakest class for a long time to come. An iron grip! With a bourgeois party that will sabotage industry and a peasant population that will burn the crops to starve us out?

HUGO: What of that? The Bolshevik Party survived worse in 1917.

HŒDERER: It wasn't imposed by a foreign power. Listen to me, son, and try to understand. We can take power with Karsky's liberals and the Regent's conservatives. No fuss, nobody hurt, a united front. No one can accuse us of having been put in by a foreign power. I demanded half the votes on the resistance committee, but I wouldn't be foolish enough to ask for half the ministries. A minority, that's what we must be. A minority, leaving to the other parties the responsibility for unpopular measures and thus able to win support by opposing these measures inside the government. They're cornered: in two years you'll see the bankruptcy of the liberals, and the whole country will ask us to take a try.

HUGO : But at that moment the party will be done for.

HŒDERER : Done for? Why?

HUGO : The party has one program: the realization of a socialist economy, and one method of achieving it: the class struggle. You are going to use it to pursue a policy of class collaboration in the framework of a capitalist economy. For years you will have to cheat, trick, and maneuver; we'll go from compromise to compromise. Before your comrades, you will have to defend the reactionary measures taken by the government in which you participate. No one will understand: the hardened ones will leave us, the others will lose whatever political faith they have just acquired. We shall be contaminated, weakened, disoriented; we shall become reformists and nationalists; in the end the bourgeois parties won't even have to go to the trouble of liquidating us. Hœderer! This party is yours, you cannot have forgotten the hardships you endured to forge it, the sacrifices that were required, the discipline you had to impose. I beg you: don't sacrifice it with your own hands.

HŒDERER : What babbling! If you don't want to take chances you shouldn't be in politics.

HUGO : I don't want to run these particular risks.

HŒDERER : Excellent. Then how would you stay in power?

HUGO : Why take it?

HŒDERER : Are you mad? A socialist army is going to

occupy the country; would you let it go without profiting by its aid? Such a chance never comes twice. I tell you we are not strong enough to swing the revolution alone.

HUGO: You should not take power at such a price.

HŒDERER: What do you think the party is, a racing stable? Why polish a knife every day if you don't intend to cut something with it? A party is always only a tool. It has only one goal: power.

HUGO: It has only one goal: to make our ideas, all our ideas, and only these victorious.

HŒDERER: That's true. Now you—you have ideas. You'll get over them.

HUGO: You think I'm the only one who has these ideas? Wasn't it for these ideas that our comrades were killed by the Regent's police? Don't you see that we'll betray them if we use the party to whitewash their assassins?

HŒDERER: I don't give a damn for the dead. They died for the party, and the party can decide as it sees fit about them. I pursue a policy of the living for the living.

HUGO: And do you think that the living will agree to your schemes?

HŒDERER: We'll get them to swallow them little by little.

HUGO: By lying to them?

HŒDERER: By lying to them sometimes.

HUGO: You—you seem so real, so solid! How can you stand it to lie to your comrades?

HŒDERER: Why not? We're at war, and it's not customary to keep each individual soldier posted hour by hour on operations.

HUGO: Hœderer, I—I know better than you what lies are like. In my father's home everybody lied to himself, everybody lied to me. I couldn't breathe until I joined the party. Then for the first time I saw men who didn't lie to other men. Everyone could have confidence in everyone else, the humblest militant had the feeling that the orders of the leaders revealed to him his own secret will, and if things got tough, each one knew why he was ready to die. You're not going to—

HŒDERER: What are you talking about?

HUGO: Our party.

HŒDERER: Our party? But we have always told lies, just like any other party. And you, Hugo, are you sure that you've never lied, never lied to yourself, that you are not even lying to me this very moment?

HUGO: I never lie to my comrades. I— Why should you fight for the liberation of men, if you think no more of them than to stuff their heads with falsehoods?

HŒDERER: I'll lie when I must, and I have contempt for no one. I wasn't the one who invented lying. It grew out of a society divided into classes, and each one of us has inherited it from birth. We shall not abolish lying by refusing to tell lies, but by using every means at hand to abolish classes.

HUGO: All means are not good.

HŒDERER: All means are good when they're effective.

HUGO: Then what right have you to condemn the policy of the Regent? He declared war on the U.S.S.R. because this was the most effective way of safeguarding national independence.

HŒDERER: Do you imagine I condemn him? He did what any fellow of his class would have done in his place. We're not fighting against men nor against a policy, but against the class that produces this policy and these men.

HUGO: And the best means you've found to fight that class is to ask it to share power with you?

HŒDERER: Right! Today it's the best means. [*A pause.*] How you cling to your purity, young man! How afraid you are to soil your hands! All right, stay pure! What good will it do? Why did you join us? Purity is an idea for a yogi or a monk. You intellectuals and bourgeois anarchists use it as a pretext for doing nothing. To do nothing, to remain motionless, arms at your sides, wearing kid gloves. Well, I have dirty hands. Right up to the elbows. I've plunged them in filth and blood. But what do you hope? Do you think you can govern innocently?

HUGO: You'll see some day that I'm not afraid of blood.

HŒDERER: Really! Red gloves, that's elegant. It's the rest that scares you. That's what stinks to your little aristocratic nose.

HUGO: So we're back to that! I'm an aristocrat, a guy who has never gone hungry. Unfortunately for you, I'm not alone in my opinion.

HŒDERER: Not alone? Then you knew something of these negotiations before you came here?

HUGO: N—no. There was some vague talk in the party,

and most of the fellows didn't agree. And I swear to you that they weren't aristocrats.

HŒDERER : My boy, you misunderstand something; I know these people of the party who disagree with my policy, and I can tell you that they belong to my tribe and not to yours—as you'll soon discover. If they oppose these negotiations, it's simply because they believe them to be inopportune; under other circumstances they would be the first to launch them. But you are making this a matter of principle.

HUGO : Who spoke of principles?

HŒDERER : Aren't you trying to make this into a matter of principle? Good. Then here is something that ought to convince you: if we deal with the Regent, he'll stop the war; the Illyrian troops will wait very patiently for the Russians to come and disarm them. If we break off these parleys, they'll know the game is off and they'll assail us like mad dogs. Hundreds of thousands of men will lose their hides. What do you say to that? [*A pause.*] Now what do you say? Can you scratch out a hundred thousand men with the stroke of a pen?

HUGO [*with difficulty*] : You can't make a revolution with flowers. If there's no other way—

HŒDERER : Then?

HUGO : Why then, so much the worse!

HŒDERER : There you are! You can see for yourself! You don't love men, Hugo. You love only principles.

HUGO : Men? Why should I love them? Do they love me?

HŒDERER : Then why did you come to us? If you don't love men, you can't fight for them.

HUGO : I joined the party because its cause is just, and I shall leave it when that cause ceases to be just. As for men, it's not what they are that interests me, but what they can become.

HŒDERER : And I, I love them for what they are. With all their filth and all their vices. I love their voices and their warm grasping hands, and their skin, the nudest skin of all, and their uneasy glances, and the desperate struggle each has to pursue against anguish and against death. For me, one man more or less in the world is something that counts. It's something precious. You, I know you now, you are a destroyer. You detest men because you detest yourself. Your purity resembles death. The revolution you dream of is not ours. You don't want to change the world, you want to blow it up.

HUGO [*excited*] : Hœderer:

HŒDERER : It's not your fault; you're all alike. An intellectual is never a real revolutionary; just good enough to make an assassin.

HUGO : An assassin. Yes!

JESSICA : Hugo! [*She slips between them.*]

[*The sound of a key in the lock. Enter* SLICK *and* GEORGE.]

GEORGE : So here you are. We've been looking all over for you.

HUGO : Who gave you my key?

SLICK : We have keys to all the doors. Remember— we're bodyguards.

GEORGE [*to* HŒDERER] : You gave us a scare. It was Slick who woke: no Hœderer. You ought to warn us when you want to go out for a breath of air.

HŒDERER : You were sleeping.

SLICK [*flustered*] : What of it? Since when do you let us sleep when you want to wake us?

HŒDERER [*laughing*] : That's right: What's got into me? [*A pause.*] I'll go along with you. Till tomorrow, son. At nine o'clock. We can talk some more then. [HUGO *does not answer.*] Good-by, Jessica.

JESSICA : Till tomorrow, Hœderer. [*They go out. A long silence.*]

JESSICA : Well?

HUGO : Well, you were here. You heard.

JESSICA : What are you thinking?

HUGO : What do you want me to think? I told you he was shrewd.

JESSICA : Hugo! He was right.

HUGO : My poor Jessica, what could you know about it?

JESSICA : And you, what do you know about it? You didn't look so big in front of him.

HUGO : Oh, for heaven's sake! With me, he had it lucky. I should like to see how he would make out with Louis. He wouldn't have come out so well.

JESSICA : Perhaps he would have put him in his pocket.

HUGO [*laughing*] : What? Louis? You don't know him. Louis can't be wrong.

JESSICA : Why?

HUGO : Because. Because he's Louis.

JESSICA : Hugo! You don't mean what you're saying.

I watched you while you were arguing with Hœderer: he convinced you.

HUGO : He didn't convince me. No one can convince me that one should lie to one's comrades. But if he had convinced me, that would be one more reason to kill him, because that would prove that he's capable of convincing others. Tomorrow morning I'll finish the job.

CURTAIN

ACT VI

HŒDERER'S OFFICE

The two torn-off sashes of the window have been leaned against the wall. The fragments of glass have been carefully swept up and the window is covered with a drape, which hangs to the floor.

At the beginning of the scene, HŒDERER *is standing in front of the gas burner, making coffee and smoking his pipe. There is a knock and* SLICK *sticks his head through the partly open door.*

SLICK : It's the dame. She wants to see you.

HŒDERER : No.

SLICK : She says it's very important.

HŒDERER : Very well. Tell her to come in.

[JESSICA *enters.* SLICK *withdraws.*] Well? [*She is silent.*] Come here. [*She remains standing by the door, her hair falling across her face. He goes up to her.*] I suppose you have something to tell me? [*She nods.*] Very well, out with it, and then make yourself scarce.

JESSICA : You're always in such a hurry.

HŒDERER : I'm working.

JESSICA : You weren't working: you're making yourself coffee. May I have a cup?

HŒDERER : Yes. [*A pause.*] Well?

JESSICA : You must give me a little time. It's so hard to talk to you. You're waiting for Hugo and he hasn't even begun to shave.

HŒDERER : All right. You have five minutes to collect yourself. Here's your coffee.

JESSICA : Talk to me.

HŒDERER : Why?

JESSICA : So I can pull myself together. Talk to me.

HŒDERER : I have nothing to say to you. I don't know how to talk to women.

JESSICA : Yes you do. And very well.

HŒDERER : Oh! [*A pause.*]

JESSICA : Last night—

HŒDERER : What about last night?

JESSICA : I discovered that you're the one who's right.

HŒDERER : Right? Oh! [*A pause.*] Thank you, I feel encouraged.

JESSICA : You are making fun of me.

HŒDERER : Yes. [*A pause.*]

JESSICA : What would they do with me if I joined the party?

HŒDERER : They would first have to let you in.

JESSICA : But if they let me in, what would they do with me?

HŒDERER : I wonder. [*A pause.*] Is that what you came to tell me?

JESSICA : No.

HŒDERER : Well then? What's wrong? Did you quarrel with Hugo and decide to walk out?

JESSICA : No. Would you be annoyed if I left?

HŒDERER: I should be delighted. I could work in peace.

JESSICA: You don't really mean that.

HŒDERER: No?

JESSICA: No. [*A pause.*] Last night when you came in, you seemed so alone in the world.

HŒDERER: And?

JESSICA: It's wonderful to see a man who stands alone.

HŒDERER: So wonderful that you at once want to keep him company. And so, just like that, he's no longer alone. The world is made badly.

JESSICA: With me you'd be quite alone. I wouldn't get in your way.

HŒDERER: With you?

JESSICA: That's a manner of speaking. [*A pause.*] Were you ever married?

HŒDERER: Yes.

JESSICA: To a woman in the party?

HŒDERER: No.

JESSICA: You said one should always marry a woman in the party.

HŒDERER: Exactly.

JESSICA: Was she beautiful?

HŒDERER: That depended on the hour and the point of view.

JESSICA: And do you think I'm beautiful?

HŒDERER: Are you making an ass of me?

JESSICA [*laughing*]: Yes.

HŒDERER: The five minutes are up. Talk or be off with you.

JESSICA: You won't hurt him.

HŒDERER : Whom?

JESSICA : Hugo! You like him, don't you?

HŒDERER : Please don't get sentimental. He means to kill me, eh? Isn't that what's on your mind?

JESSICA : Don't harm him.

HŒDERER : Of course I shan't hurt him.

JESSICA : You—you've known?

HŒDERER : Since yesterday. How does he intend to kill me?

JESSICA : How?

HŒDERER : With what weapon? Hand-grenade, revolver, pickax, dagger, or poison?

JESSICA : Revolver.

HŒDERER : I prefer that.

JESSICA : When he comes in this morning he'll have his revolver on him.

HŒDERER : Good. Good, good. But why do you betray him? Are you angry with him?

JESSICA : No. But—

HŒDERER : Well?

JESSICA : He asked me to help him.

HŒDERER : And this is how you go about helping him? You surprise me.

JESSICA : He doesn't want to kill you. Not in the least. He thinks too much of you for that. It's just that he has his assignment. He won't admit it, but I know that at the bottom of his heart he would be happy if he were prevented from carrying it out.

HŒDERER : That remains to be seen.

JESSICA : What are you going to do?

HŒDERER : I don't know yet.

◇◇

JESSICA : Have him disarmed gently by Slick. He has just that gun. Once the gun is gone, it will be all over.

HŒDERER : No. That would humiliate him. One shouldn't humiliate a man. I'll talk to him.

JESSICA : You are going to let him come in here armed?

HŒDERER : Why not? I want to win him over. It will be risky for five minutes, but not after that. If he doesn't go through with it this morning, he'll never do it.

JESSICA [*abruptly*] : I don't want him to kill you.

HŒDERER : Would you care if I got killed?

JESSICA : I? I should be delighted.

[*A knock.*]

SLICK : It's Hugo.

HŒDERER : Just a minute. [SLICK *closes the door.*] Go out by the window.

JESSICA : I don't want to leave you.

HŒDERER : If you stay he's certain to shoot. In front of you he wouldn't back down. Come on, get out! [*She goes out through the window, and the drape falls back into place.*]

HŒDERER : Let him in.

[HUGO *enters.* HŒDERER *goes to the door and follows* HUGO *to the table. He stays close to him, observing all his gestures while they talk, ready to seize his wrists if* HUGO *should reach for the gun in his pocket.*]

HŒDERER : Did you sleep well?

HUGO : All right.

HŒDERER : Hangover?

HUGO : Awful.

HŒDERER : Did you make up your mind?

HUGO [*startled*] : To do what?

HŒDERER : You told me yesterday you would leave me if you were unable to make me change my views.

HUGO : I still feel the same way.

HŒDERER : Good. But we'll talk about that later. Meantime let's do some work. Sit down. [HUGO *sits at the work-table.*] Where were we?

HUGO [*reading his notes*] : "According to official figures the number of agricultural workers fell in 1906 from 8,771,000 to—"

HŒDERER : Tell me: did you know that it was a woman who threw the bomb?

HUGO : A woman?

HŒDERER : Slick saw footprints in a flowerbed. Did you know her?

HUGO : How should I know her? [*A pause.*]

HŒDERER : It's strange, isn't it?

HUGO : Very.

HŒDERER : But you don't really seem to think it's strange. What's the matter with you?

HUGO : I'm sick.

HŒDERER : Would you like to take the morning off?

HUGO : No. Let's work.

HŒDERER : Then finish that sentence.

HUGO [*takes up his notes and begins again to read*] : "According to official statistics—" [HŒDERER *begins to laugh.* HUGO *raises his head sharply.*]

HŒDERER : Do you know why she missed us? I'll bet she shut her eyes when she threw the bomb.

HUGO [*absent-mindedly*] : Why?

HŒDERER : Because of the noise. They close their eyes so as not to hear it; explain it any way you like. Women are all afraid of loud noises, the little mice, otherwise they'd make remarkable killers. They're pigheaded, you know. They get their ideas ready-made, and then they believe in them as in God. With us others, it's not so easy for us to shoot some chap for the sake of a theory, because we're the ones who cook up the theories and we know how they are made. We can never be entirely certain that we're right. Take you: are you sure you're right?

HUGO : Yes.

HŒDERER : In any case, you'll never make a killer; it's a vocation.

HUGO : Anyone can kill if the party orders him to.

HŒDERER : If the party ordered you to dance on a tight-rope, do you think you would succeed? One has to be born a killer. Take you, you think too much; you couldn't do it.

HUGO : I could if I made up my mind.

HŒDERER : You could coldly put a bullet between my eyes because I don't agree with your political views?

HUGO : Yes, if I had decided to or if the party had ordered it.

HŒDERER : You surprise me. [HUGO *is about to reach into his pocket, but* HŒDERER *grabs his arm and lifts it lightly above the table.*] Suppose this arm were clasping a gun and the finger rested on the trigger.

HUGO : Let go of my hand.

HŒDERER [*not releasing it*] : Suppose I were facing you, just as now, and you took aim.

HUGO : Let me go and let's get to work.

HŒDERER : You would look at me and just as you were all set to fire, this is what would come into your mind: "What if he were right?" Don't you see?

HUGO : I wouldn't think of that. I would only think of killing.

HŒDERER : You would think of that. Being an intellectual, you can't keep from thinking. Before pulling the trigger you would have already seen all the possible consequences of your act: the work of a lifetime in ruins, a policy gone to pot, nobody to replace me, the party condemned, maybe, never to take power—

HUGO : I tell you I would think no such thing!

HŒDERER : You couldn't help yourself. And rightly so, for if you didn't think of it beforehand, a whole lifetime of thinking would not be enough for you afterwards. [*A pause.*] What's this mania that you all have to play the assassin? Your killer is a guy without imagination: he doesn't give a damn for death because he has no idea of what life is. I prefer people who fear the death of others: it shows they know how to live.

HUGO : I'm not built for living, I don't know what life is and I don't need to know. I'm in the way, I haven't found the right place for myself and I get on everyone's nerves. Nobody loves me, nobody trusts me.

HŒDERER : *I* trust you.

HUGO : You?

HŒDERER : Certainly. You're a kid for whom the passage to maturity is not easy, but you'll make a fair enough man if somebody helps you over the hump. If I escape their bombs I'll keep you with me and help you.

HUGO : Why do you tell me this? Why tell it to me today?

HŒDERER [*releasing him*] : Simply to prove to you that you can't drop a man in cold blood unless you're a specialist.

HUGO : If I decided to, I should be able to do it. [*To himself, with a kind of desperation*] I should be able to do it.

HŒDERER : Could you face me and fire? [*They face each other.* HUGO *backs his chair away from the table.*] Your real killer has no notion of what the other one is thinking. But you have a very good notion. Could you bear to know what I would be thinking as I saw you take aim? [*A pause.* HŒDERER *keeps watching* HUGO.] Would you like some coffee? [HUGO *doesn't answer.*] It's ready; I'll get you a cup. [*He turns his back on* HUGO *and pours a cup of coffee.* HUGO *gets up from his chair and reaches into the pocket that holds his revolver. It is clear that he is struggling with himself. After a moment* HŒDERER *turns around and calmly approaches* HUGO, *carrying a full cup. He offers it to him.*] Take it. [HUGO *takes the cup.*] And now give me your gun. Give it to me! I gave you your chance and you didn't take it. [*He reaches into* HUGO's *pocket and takes out the revolver.*] Why, it's a plaything! [*He goes to his desk and deposits the gun.*]

HUGO : I hate you. [HŒDERER *comes up to him.*]

HŒDERER : No, you don't hate me. What reason have you to hate me?

HUGO : You take me for a coward.

HŒDERER : Why? You don't know how to kill, but that doesn't mean that you don't know how to die. On the contrary.

HUGO : I had my finger on the trigger.

HŒDERER : Yes.

HUGO : And I—[*with a gesture of helplessness*].

HŒDERER : Yes. I told you: it's harder than you think.

HUGO : I knew that you were deliberately turning your back. That was why—

HŒDERER : Oh! In any case—

HUGO : I'm not a traitor!

HŒDERER : Who said anything about that? Treachery, too, is a vocation.

HUGO : They'll think I'm a traitor because I didn't do as I was instructed.

HŒDERER : Who? They? [*Silence.*] It's Louis who sent you? [*Silence.*] You won't say. That's as it should be. [*A pause.*] Listen to me: your fate is linked with mine. Since yesterday I have some trump cards, and I'm going to try to save both our necks. Tomorrow I'll go to the city and talk to Louis. He's tough, but then so am I. We can square it with your pals easily enough. The difficult thing for you will be to square it with yourself.

HUGO : Not so difficult. Just give me back the gun.

HŒDERER : No.

HUGO : What's it to you if I put a bullet in my head? I'm your enemy.

HŒDERER : First of all you're not my enemy. And then, too, you can still be of use.

HUGO : You know that I'm washed up!

HŒDERER : Nonsense! You wanted to prove that you were capable of acting and you chose the hard way, as if you wanted to gather up credit in heaven; that's youth. You didn't succeed. Well, what of that? There's nothing to prove, you know, and the revolution's not a question of virtue but of effectiveness. There is no heaven. There's work to be done, that's all. And you must do what you're cut out for; all the better if it comes easy to you. The best work is not the work that takes the most sacrifices. It's the work in which you can best succeed.

HUGO : I have no gift for anything.

HŒDERER : You have a gift for writing.

HUGO : For writing! Words! Always words!

HŒDERER : And why not? The point is to succeed. Better a good journalist than a poor assassin.

HUGO [*hesitating, but with a kind of confidence*] : Hœderer, when you were my age—

HŒDERER : Yes?

HUGO : What would you have done in my place?

HŒDERER : I? I should have killed my man. But that doesn't mean I should have done the best thing. But then, we are not of the same tribe.

HUGO : I would rather belong to your tribe; you must feel right inside.

HŒDERER : You think so? [*He laughs dryly.*] Some day I'll tell you about me.

HUGO : Some day? [*A pause.*] Hœderer, I missed my chance, and I know now that I could never shoot you because—because I like you. But make no mistake about it: on the question we discussed yesterday I shall never agree with you, I shall never be on your side and I don't want you to defend me. Not tomorrow nor any other day.

HŒDERER : As you like.

HUGO : And now may I have your permission to leave? I'd like to think this whole thing over.

HŒDERER : Will you give me your word that you won't do anything foolish until you have talked with me again?

HUGO : If you like.

HŒDERER : Then go on. Get some fresh air and come back as soon as you can. And don't forget that you're still my secretary. So long as you don't shoot me and I don't fire you, you'll work for me.

[HUGO *goes out.* HŒDERER *goes to the door.*]

HŒDERER : Slick!

SLICK : Yes?

HŒDERER : The kid's unhappy. Keep an eye on him from a distance, and if necessary, keep him from doing himself any mischief. But be nice about it. And if he wants to come back here in a little while, don't stop him on the pretext that you have to announce him. Let him go and come as he pleases. The important thing is not to excite him.

[*He shuts the door and goes to the table on which*

the gas burner is sitting. He pours himself a cup of coffee. JESSICA *lifts the hanging that covers the window and comes in.*]

HŒDERER: You again, you poison? What do you want now?

JESSICA: I was sitting on the window-ledge and I heard everything.

HŒDERER: Well?

JESSICA: I was frightened.

HŒDERER: You didn't have to stay.

JESSICA: I couldn't leave you.

HŒDERER: You wouldn't have been much help.

JESSICA: I know. [*A pause.*] Maybe I would have thrown myself in between you and got the bullets meant for you.

HŒDERER: You're a romantic.

JESSICA: So are you.

HŒDERER: What?

JESSICA: You are romantic too: you risked your life rather than humiliate him.

HŒDERER: To know what life is worth you have to risk it once in a while.

JESSICA: You offered to help him and he refused and yet you were not discouraged. You actually seemed to be fond of him.

HŒDERER: What of it?

JESSICA: Nothing. That's how it was, that's all. [*They look at each other.*]

HŒDERER: Now beat it! [*She doesn't budge.*] Jessica, I'm not in the habit of refusing what is offered me, and it's six months since I've touched a woman. You still have time to go, but in five minutes it will be too late. Do you understand what I mean? [*She doesn't budge.*] The boy has only you in the world and he has all sorts of trouble ahead of him. He needs someone to give him courage.

JESSICA: You're the one who can give him courage. Not me. We can only harm each other.

HŒDERER: You love each other.

JESSICA: Not even. We're too much alike. [*A pause.*]

HŒDERER: When did this start?

JESSICA: What?

HŒDERER [*with a gesture*]: All this. All this in your head.

JESSICA: I don't know. Yesterday, I think when you looked at me and seemed so alone.

HŒDERER: If I had known—

JESSICA: You wouldn't have come?

HŒDERER: I— [*He looks at her and shrugs his shoulders. A pause.*] But good God! If you're restless, there are Slick and George to distract you. Why pick me?

JESSICA: I'm not restless and I didn't pick anyone. I didn't have to pick.

HŒDERER: You bother me. [*A pause.*] What did you expect? I don't have the time to worry with you. You don't expect me to give you a toss on that sofa and then abandon you afterwards, do you?

JESSICA: Make up your mind.

HŒDERER: Just the same, you ought to know—

JESSICA: I don't know anything. I'm not a girl, but I'm not a woman either. I've lived in a dream, and when

I was kissed I always wanted to laugh. And now that I am standing here in front of you, it seems to me that the morning has come and that I just woke up. You are real. A real man of flesh and bone. I am actually afraid of you and I think I really love you. Do whatever you like with me. No matter what happens, I'll not complain.

HŒDERER: You felt like laughing when you were kissed? [JESSICA, *embarrassed, lowers her head.*] Eh?

JESSICA: Yes.

HŒDERER: Why? Are you cold?

JESSICA: That's what they say.

HOŒDERER: And you, what's your opinion?

JESSICA: I don't know.

HŒDERER: Well, let's just see. [*He kisses her.*] Well?

JESSICA: I didn't feel like laughing. [*The door opens.* HUGO *enters.*]

HUGO: So that's the way it is!

HŒDERER: Hugo—

HUGO: That's enough. [*A pause.*] So that's why you spared me. I wondered why you didn't have your men beat me up and throw me out. I said to myself: he can't be so mad or so generous. But it's all clear now: it was on account of my wife. I like it better this way.

JESSICA: Listen to me.

HUGO: Never mind, Jessica, forget it. I'm not sore at you and I'm not jealous; we weren't really in love. But he, he almost took me in: "I'll help you, I'll help make a man of you." What a fool I was! He didn't give a damn for me.

HŒDERER : Hugo, do you want me to swear that—

HUGO : Above all, don't apologize. On the contrary, I should thank you. At least once I've had the pleasure of catching you in a bad moment. And besides— besides— [*He rushes to the desk, snatches up the revolver, and covers* HŒDERER.] And besides, you have freed me.

JESSICA [*shouting*] : Hugo!

HUGO : You see, Hœderer, I am looking you straight in the eyes and I'm aiming and my hand's not shaking and I don't give a bloody damn for what's going on in your head.

HŒDERER : Wait, kid! Don't be stupid. Not for a woman! [HUGO *fires three shots.* JESSICA *screams.* SLICK *and* GEORGE *rush in.*] You imbecile! You've ruined everything.

SLICK : You bastard! [*He draws his revolver.*]

HŒDERER : Don't hurt him. [*He sinks into a chair.*] He was jealous. That's why he shot me.

SLICK : What's that mean?

HŒDERER : I've been sleeping with his wife. [*A pause.*] What a god-damn waste!
[*He dies.*]

CURTAIN

ACT VII

IN OLGA'S ROOM

OLGA *and* HUGO *talking in the dark. First their voices are heard, and then gradually the room is lighted.*

OLGA : Was it true? Did you really kill him over Jessica?

HUGO : I—I killed him because I opened the door. That's all I know. If I hadn't opened that door— He was there, he held Jessica in his arms, he had lipstick on his chin. It was all so trivial. But I had been living for so long in tragedy. It was to save the tragedy that I fired.

OLGA : But weren't you jealous?

HUGO : Jealous? Perhaps. But not about Jessica.

OLGA : Look at me and answer me frankly, for what I am going to ask now is very important. Are you proud of your deed? Do you claim it as your own? Would you do it again if necessary?

HUGO : Did I even do it? It wasn't I who killed—it was chance. If I had opened the door two minutes sooner or two minutes later, I wouldn't have surprised them in each other's arms, and I wouldn't have fired. [*A pause.*] I was coming to tell him that I would let him help me.

OLGA : Yes.

HUGO : Chance fired three shots, just as in cheap detective stories. Chance lets you do a lot of "iffing": "*If* I had stayed a bit longer by the chestnut trees, *if* I had walked to the end of the garden, *if* I had gone back into the summerhouse. . . ." But me? *Me?* Where does that put me in the thing? It was an assassination without an assassin. [*A pause.*] I often asked myself in prison: what would Olga say if she were here? What would she want me to think?

OLGA [*dryly*] : Well?

HUGO : Oh, I know perfectly well what you would have said to me. You would have said: "Be modest, Hugo. Nobody cares about your motives or reasons. We asked you to kill this man and you killed him. What counts is the result." But I—well, I'm not modest, Olga. I can't separate the murder from the motive for it.

OLGA : I like that better.

HUGO : What do you mean, you like that better? Is that really you talking, Olga? The Olga who always told me that—

OLGA : I'll explain. What time is it?

HUGO [*looking at his wrist watch*] : Twenty minutes to twelve.

OLGA : Good. We have time. What were you saying? That you do not understand your deed.

HUGO : Rather, that I understand it too well. It's a door that any key can open. I could tell myself, if I had a mind to, that I shot him out of political passion and that the rage that came over me when I opened the door was merely the little jolt I needed to make my task easier.

OLGA [*observing him with uneasiness*] : Do you believe that, Hugo? Do you really believe that you fired for the right reasons?

HUGO : Olga, I believe everything. And at the same time I wonder whether I really killed him at all.

OLGA : What do you mean—at all?

HUGO : What if it were all a comedy?

OLGA : You really pulled the trigger.

HUGO : Yes. I really drew my finger back. Actors do that too, on the stage. Look here: I cock my fore-finger, I aim at you. [*He aims at her with his right hand, his forefinger coiled back.*] It's the same ges-ture. Perhaps I wasn't real. Perhaps only the bullet was. Why do you smile?

OLGA : Because you make many things easy for me.

HUGO : I thought I was too young. I wanted to hang a crime round my neck, like a stone. And I feared it would be too heavy for me to carry. How wrong I was! It's light, horribly light. It has no weight at all. Look at me: I've grown older, I spent two years in the cooler, I've been separated from Jessica, and I shall lead this life of senseless puzzlement until your pals take it upon themselves to rid me of it. And all this comes from my crime, isn't that right? And yet it has no weight, I don't feel that it's there. It's not around my neck, nor on my shoulders, nor in my heart. It has become my destiny, do you understand? It controls my life from outside, but I can't see it or touch it, it's not mine, it's a fatal disease that kills painlessly. Where is my crime? Does it exist? And yet I fired. The door was open. I loved Hœderer, Olga. I loved him more than I ever loved anyone in the world. I loved to watch him and to hear him talk, I loved his hands and his face, and when I was with him all my fears were calmed. It's not my crime that tortures me but the fact that he's dead. [*A pause.*] So there you are. Nothing happened. Nothing. I spent ten days in the country and two years in jail; I haven't changed; I'm still the same old chatterbox. Assassins should wear something by which they can be recognized. A poppy in their lapels. [*A pause.*] Well, then? What's the conclusion?

OLGA: You're coming back to the party.

HUGO: Good.

OLGA: At midnight Louis and Charles will return to kill you. But I won't let them in. I'll tell them you are salvageable.

HUGO [*laughs*]: Salvageable! What an odd word! That's a word you use for scrap, isn't it?

OLGA: Do you agree?

HUGO: Why not?

OLGA: Tomorrow you'll get new instructions.

HUGO: Good.

OLGA: Thank heaven! [*She sinks into a chair.*]

HUGO: What's wrong with you?

OLGA: I'm so glad. [*A pause.*] You talked for three hours and I was frightened all that time.

HUGO: What were you afraid of?

OLGA: Of what I might have had to tell them. But

everything is all right now. You'll come back with us now and do a man's work.

HUGO: Will you help me, as before?

OLGA: Yes, Hugo, I'll help you.

HUGO: I do like you, Olga. You are just as you always were. So pure, so clear. It was you who taught me purity.

OLGA: Have I aged?

HUGO: No. [*He takes her hand.*]

OLGA: I thought of you every day.

HUGO: Tell me, Olga—

OLGA: Yes?

HUGO: About those packages. Did you send them?

OLGA: What packages?

HUGO: The chocolates.

OLGA: No. It wasn't I. But I knew they were going to send them.

HUGO: And you let them?

OLGA: Yes.

HUGO: But what did you think about it?

OLGA [*showing her hair*]: Look.

HUGO: What's this? White hairs?

OLGA: They came in one night. You must never leave me again. And if there are rough times we'll manage them together.

HUGO [*smiling*]: You remember: Raskolnikov.

OLGA [*leaping to her feet*]: Raskolnikov?

HUGO: It's the name you chose for me in the underground. Oh, Olga, you don't remember!

OLGA: Yes. I remember.

HUGO: I'll use it again.

OLGA: No.

HUGO: Why? I liked it. You said it fitted me like a glove.

OLGA: You're too well known under that name.

HUGO: Known? By whom?

OLGA [*suddenly limp*]: What time is it?

HUGO: Five minutes to.

OLGA: Listen carefully, Hugo. And don't interrupt. I have something to tell you. It isn't much. You mustn't attach any importance to it. You—you'll be surprised at first, but you'll come to understand after a while.

HUGO: Well?

OLGA: I'm happy about what you told me, about your —about your deed. If you had taken pride in it or spoken of it with satisfaction, it would have been more difficult for you.

HUGO: Difficult? Difficult to do what?

OLGA: To forget it.

HUGO: To forget it? But, Olga—

OLGA: Hugo! You must forget it. I'm not asking much of you; you said yourself that you didn't know what you were doing or why you did it. You're not even sure that you killed Hœderer. Very good, you're on the right track. You've got to go just a bit farther, that's all. Forget it; it was a nightmare. Never mention it again; not even to me. The man who killed Hœderer is dead. He was known as Raskolnikov, and he died of eating some poisoned brandy-chocolates. [*She strokes his hair.*] I'll choose another name for you.

◇◇

HUGO : What's going on here, Olga? What have you done?

OLGA : The party has changed its policy. [HUGO *regards her fixedly*.] Don't look at me like that. Try to understand. When we sent you to Hœderer's our communications with the Soviet Union were severed. We had to decide our line by ourselves. Don't look at me that way, Hugo. Don't look at me like that.

HUGO : Then what?

OLGA : Then the contact was renewed. Last winter the U.S.S.R. informed us that for purely military reasons it favored a policy of conciliation with the Regent.

HUGO : And you—did you obey?

OLGA : Yes. We set up a secret committee of six members with the government people and the Pentagon.

HUGO : Six members? And you have three votes?

OLGA : Yes. How did you know?

HUGO : It came into my head, somehow. Go on.

OLGA : Since then our troops have been practically out of the war. We've probably saved a hundred thousand lives. Except that the Germans immediately invaded the country.

HUGO : Just perfect. I suppose the Russians also gave you to understand that they didn't want to give sole power to the Proletarian Party; that they would have trouble with the Allies and that, what's more, you would soon be swept out by an insurrection?

OLGA : But—

HUGO : I seem to have heard all that once before. What about Hœderer?

OLGA : His attempt was premature and he was not the right man to direct such a policy.

HUGO : So he had to be killed; that's clear. But I suppose you have rehabilitated his reputation?

OLGA : We had to.

HUGO : He'll have a statue to him at the end of the war, and streets named after him in all our cities, and his name in the history books. That makes me happy for him. And who was his assassin? What was he? Some character in the pay of Germany?

OLGA : Hugo—

HUGO : Answer me.

OLGA : The comrades know that you were one of us. They never believed it was a crime of passion. Then it was explained to them—as best it could be.

HUGO : You've lied to your comrades.

OLGA : Lied, no. But we—we are at war, Hugo. You can't tell the whole truth to troops. [HUGO *bursts into laughter.*] What is the matter? Hugo! Hugo!

[HUGO *sinks into a chair, laughing to the point of tears.*]

HUGO : That's just what he said! Just what he said! Oh, this is a farce.

OLGA : Hugo!

HUGO : Wait, Olga, let me have my laugh. It's been ten years since I've been able to laugh like this. Here's an embarrassing crime: nobody wants to claim it. I don't know why I committed it and you don't know what to do with it. [*He looks at her.*] You're all alike.

OLGA : Hugo, I beg you—

HUGO : Alike. Hœderer, Louis, and you yourself, all belong to the same tribe. The right tribe. You're the tough ones, the conquerors, the leaders. I am the only one who got in by the wrong door.

OLGA : Hugo, you loved Hœderer.

HUGO : I believe I never before loved him as much as I do at this moment.

OLGA : Then you must help us complete his work. [*She recoils under his glance.*] Hugo!

HUGO [*softly*] : Don't be afraid, Olga. I'll not harm you. But you must be quiet. For one minute, just for one minute more, while I put my thoughts in order. Good. So I am salvageable. Excellent. But all alone, naked, without bag or baggage. On condition that I change my skin—if I could develop amnesia, that would be better still. The crime itself cannot be salvaged, isn't that so? It was an error of no significance. To be left in the ash-can. As for me, I'll change my name tomorrow, call myself Julien Sorel or Rastignac or Muishkin, and I'll work hand in hand with the guys of the Pentagon.

OLGA : I'm going—

HUGO : Quiet, Olga. I beg you, don't say a word. [*He reflects a moment.*] The answer is no.

OLGA : What?

HUGO : My answer is no. I won't work with you.

OLGA : Then you can't have understood, Hugo. They're coming with their revolvers—

HUGO : I understand perfectly well. They're even a little late.

OLGA : You're not going to let them kill you like a dog.
You can't be willing to die for nothing! We will
trust you, Hugo. You'll see, you'll be our comrade
for good, you have proved yourself. . . . [*A car.
The sound of a motor.*]

HUGO : Here they are.

OLGA : Hugo, it would be criminal. The party—

HUGO : No big words, Olga. There are too many big
words in this story already and they've done much
harm. [*The car passes on.*] It's not their car. I have
time to explain it to you. Listen: I don't know why I
killed Hœderer, but I know why it was right to kill
him: because his policy was wrong, because he lied
to the rank and file and jeopardized the life of the
party. If I had had the courage to shoot when I was
alone with him in his office, he would be dead for
these reasons and I could think of myself without
shame. But I am ashamed because I killed him—
afterwards. And now you want me to dishonor myself even more and to agree that I killed him for
nothing. Olga, what I thought about Hœderer's line
I continue to think. When I was in prison I believed
that you agreed with me, and that's what kept me
going. I know now that I'm alone in my opinion, but
I won't change. [*The sound of a motor.*]

OLGA : This time they're here. Listen, I can't—take this
revolver, go out through my bedroom and make a
try.

HUGO [*not taking the gun*] : You have made Hœderer
a great man. But I loved him more than you could
ever love him. If I renounced my deed he would be-

come a nameless corpse, a throw-off of the party. [*The car stops.*] Killed by accident. Killed over a woman.

OLGA : Get out of here.

HUGO : A man like Hœderer doesn't die by accident. He dies for his ideas, for his political program; he's responsible for his death. If I openly claim my crime and declare myself Raskolnikov and am willing to pay the necessary price, then he will have the death he deserves. [*A rap on the door.*]

OLGA : Hugo, I—

HUGO [*going to the door*] : I have not yet killed Hœderer, Olga. Not yet. But I am going to kill him now, along with myself. [*More knocking.*]

OLGA [*shouting*] : Go on! Get out!

[HUGO *kicks open the door.*]

HUGO [*shouting*] : Unsalvageable!

CURTAIN

THE RESPECTFUL
PROSTITUTE

(*La Putain respectueuse*)

A PLAY IN ONE ACT AND TWO SCENES

◇◇◇

To Michel and Zette Leiris

CHARACTERS IN THE PLAY

LIZZIE

THE NEGRO

FRED

JOHN

JAMES

THE SENATOR

SEVERAL MEN

La Putain respectueuse (*The Respectful Prostitute*) was presented for the first time at the Théâtre Antoine, Paris, on November 8, 1946.

◇◇◇◇◇◇◇◇◇◇◇◇◇◇◇◇◇◇◇◇◇◇◇◇◇◇◇◇◇◇◇◇◇◇◇◇◇◇

THE RESPECTFUL PROSTITUTE

◇◇◇◇◇◇◇◇◇◇◇◇◇◇◇◇◇◇◇◇◇◇◇◇◇◇◇◇◇◇◇◇◇◇◇◇◇◇

SCENE ONE

A room in a Southern town of the United States. White walls. A couch. To the right, a window; to the left, a bathroom door. In the background, a small ante-chamber leading to the street.

Before the curtain rises, a roaring noise from the stage. LIZZIE *is alone, half dressed, running the vacuum cleaner. The bell rings. She hesitates, looks toward the door leading to the bathroom. The bell rings again. She turns off the vacuum cleaner, goes to the bathroom door, and half opens it.*

LIZZIE [*in a low voice*] : Someone is ringing, don't come out. [*She goes to open the door leading to the street.* THE NEGRO *appears in the doorway. He is a tall, strapping Negro with white hair. He stands stiffly.*] What is it? You must have the wrong address. [*A pause.*] What do you want? Speak up.

THE NEGRO [*pleading*] : Please, ma'am, please.

LIZZIE : Please what? [*She looks him over.*] Wait a

minute. That was you on the train, wasn't it? So you
got away from them, eh? How did you find my
place?

THE NEGRO: I looked, ma'am, I looked for it everywhere. [*He motions for permission to enter the
room.*] Please!

LIZZIE: Don't come in. I have somebody here. What
do you want, anyway?

THE NEGRO: Please.

LIZZIE: Please what? What? Do you want money?

THE NEGRO: No, ma'am. [*A pause.*] Please tell them
that I didn't do anything.

LIZZIE: Tell who?

THE NEGRO: The judge. Tell him, ma'am, please tell
him.

LIZZIE: I'll tell him nothing.

THE NEGRO: Please.

LIZZIE: Nothing doing. I'm not buying anybody else's
troubles, I got enough of my own. Beat it.

THE NEGRO: You know I didn't do anything. Did I do
something?

LIZZIE: Nothing. But I'm not going to the judge.
Judges and cops make me sick.

THE NEGRO: I left my wife and children. I've been running and dodging all night. I'm dead beat.

LIZZIE: Get out of town.

THE NEGRO: They're watching all the stations.

LIZZIE: Who's watching?

THE NEGRO: The white folks.

LIZZIE: Which white folks?

THE NEGRO: All of them. Were you out this morning?

LIZZIE: No.

THE NEGRO: The streets are full of all kinds of white folks. Old ones, young ones; they talk without even knowing each other.

LIZZIE: What does that mean?

THE NEGRO: It means all I can do is run around until they get me. When white folks who have never met before, start to talk to each other, friendly like, it means some nigger's goin' to die. [*A pause.*] Say I haven't done anything, ma'am. Tell the judge; tell the newspaper people. Maybe they'll print it. Tell them, ma'am, tell them, tell them!

LIZZIE: Don't shout. I got somebody here. [*A pause.*] Newspapers are out of the question. I can't afford to call attention to myself right now. [*A pause.*] If they force me to testify, I promise to tell the truth.

THE NEGRO: Are you gonna tell them I haven't done anything?

LIZZIE: I'll tell them.

THE NEGRO: You swear, ma'am?

LIZZIE: Yes, yes.

THE NEGRO: By our Lord, who sees us all?

LIZZIE: Oh, get the hell out of here. I promise, that ought to be enough. [*A pause.*] But get going. Get out!

THE NEGRO [*suddenly*]: Please, won't you hide me?

LIZZIE: Hide you?

THE NEGRO: Won't you, ma'am? Won't you?

LIZZIE: Hide you! Me? I'll show you! [*She slams the door in his face.*] And that's that! [*She turns toward the bathroom.*] You can come out.

[FRED *emerges in shirt sleeves, without collar or tie.*]

FRED : Who was that?

LIZZIE : Nobody.

FRED : I thought it was the police.

LIZZIE : The police? Are you mixed up with the police?

FRED : Me? No. I thought they came for you.

LIZZIE [*offended*] : You got a nerve! I never took a cent off anyone!

FRED : Weren't you ever in trouble with the police?

LIZZIE : Not for stealing, anyway. [*She busies herself with the vacuum cleaner.*]

FRED [*irritated by the noise*] : Hey!

LIZZIE [*shouting to make herself heard*] : What's the matter, honey?

FRED [*shouting*] : You're busting my eardrums.

LIZZIE [*shouting*] : I'll soon be finished. [*A pause.*] That's the way I am.

FRED [*shouting*] : What?

LIZZIE [*shouting*] : I tell you I'm like that.

FRED [*shouting*] : Like what?

LIZZIE [*shouting*] : Like that. I can't help it, the next morning I have to take a bath and run the vacuum cleaner. [*She leaves the vacuum cleaner.*]

FRED [*pointing toward the bed*] : Cover that, while you're at it.

LIZZIE : What?

FRED : The bed. I said you should cover the bed. It smells of sin.

LIZZIE: Sin? How come you talk like that? Are you a preacher?

FRED: No. Why?

LIZZIE: You sound like the Bible. [*She looks at him.*] No, you're not a preacher: you're too well dressed. Let's see your rings. [*Admiringly*] Say—look at that! Are you rich?

FRED: Yes.

LIZZIE: Very rich?

FRED: Yes, very.

LIZZIE: So much the better. [*She puts her arms around his neck and holds up her lips to be kissed.*] It's better when a man is rich; you feel more secure that way. [*He is about to embrace her, then turns away.*]

FRED: Cover the bed.

LIZZIE: All right, all right. I'll cover it. [*She covers the bed and laughs to herself.*] "It smells of sin!" What do you know about that? You know, it's *your* sin, honey. [FRED *shakes his head.*] Yes, of course, it's mine too. But then, I've got so many on my conscience— [*She sits down on the bed and forces* FRED *to sit beside her.*] Come on. Sit on *our* sin. A pretty nice sin, wasn't it? [*She laughs.*] But don't lower your eyes like that. Do I frighten you? [FRED *crushes her against him brutally.*] You're hurting me! You're hurting me! [*He releases her.*] You're a funny guy. You seem to be in a bad mood. [*After a while*] Tell me your first name. You don't want to? That bothers me, not to know your first name. Really, it would be the first time. They don't usually tell me their last names, and I can understand that. But the first name! How do you expect me to know one of you from another if I don't know your first names? Tell me, honey, go on.

FRED : No.

LIZZIE : Well, then, you can be the nameless gentleman. [*She gets up.*] Wait. I'm going to finish straightening things up. [*She puts a few things in order.*] There we are. Everything's in place. The chairs around the table: that's more refined. Do you know anyone who sells prints? I'd like some pictures on the wall. I have a lovely one in my trunk. *The Broken Pitcher*, it's called. It shows a young girl; she's broken her pitcher, poor thing. It's French.

FRED : What pitcher?

LIZZIE : How should I know? Her pitcher. She must have had a pitcher. I'd like to have an old grandmother to match. She could be knitting, or telling her grandchildren a story. I think I'll pull up the shades and open the window. [*She does.*] How nice it is outside! It's going to be a fine day. [*She stretches.*] Oh, I feel good; it's a beautiful day, I've taken a bath, I've had good loving; gee, I feel swell! How good I do feel! Come look at the view I have. Look! I have a lovely view. Nothing but trees, it makes you feel rich. I certainly had luck: right off I found a room in a nice place. Aren't you coming? Don't you like your own town?

FRED : I like it from my own window.

LIZZIE [*suddenly*] : It doesn't bring bad luck, to see a nigger just after waking up, does it?

FRED: Why?

LIZZIE: I—there's one going past down there, on the other side of the street.

FRED: It's always bad luck when you see a nigger. Niggers are the Devil. [*A pause.*] Close the window.

LIZZIE: Don't you want me to air the place?

FRED: I told you to close the window. O.K. And pull down the shade. Put the lights on again.

LIZZIE: Why? Because of the niggers?

FRED: Don't be stupid!

LIZZIE: It's so nice and sunny.

FRED: I don't want any sunshine in here. I want it to be like it was last night. Close the window, I said. I'll find the sunshine again when I go out. [*He gets up, goes toward her, and looks at her.*]

LIZZIE [*vaguely uneasy*]: What's the matter?

FRED: Nothing. Give me my tie.

LIZZIE: It's in the bathroom. [*She goes out.* FRED *hastily opens the drawers of the table and rummages through them.* LIZZIE *comes back with his tie.*] Here you are! Wait. [*She ties it for him.*] You know, I don't usually take one-night stands because then I have to see too many new faces. What I'd like would be to have three or four older men, one for Tuesday, one for Thursday, one for the week end. I'm telling you this: you're rather young, but you are a serious fellow, and should you ever feel the urge— Well, well, I won't insist. Think it over. My, my! You're as pretty as a picture. Kiss me, good-looking; kiss me just for the hell of it. What's the matter?

Don't you want to kiss me? [*He kisses her suddenly and brutally, then pushes her away.*] Oof!

FRED : You're the Devil.

LIZZIE : What?

FRED : You're the Devil.

LIZZIE : The Bible again! What's the matter with you?

FRED : Nothing. I was just kidding.

LIZZIE : Funny way to kid. [*A pause.*] Did you like it?

FRED : Like what?

LIZZIE [*she mimics him, smiling*] : Like what? My, but you're stupid, my little lady.

FRED : Oh! Oh that? Yes, I liked it. I liked it fine. How much do you want?

LIZZIE : Who said anything about that? I asked you if you liked it. You might have answered me nicely. What's the matter? You didn't really like it? Oh, that would surprise me, you know, that would surprise me very much.

FRED : Shut up.

LIZZIE : You held me tight, so tight. And then you whispered that you loved me.

FRED : You were drunk.

LIZZIE : No, I was not drunk.

FRED : Yes, you were drunk.

LIZZIE : I tell you I wasn't.

FRED : In any case, I was. I don't remember anything.

LIZZIE : That's a pity. I got undressed in the bathroom, and when I came back to you, you got all red and flustered, don't you remember? I even said to you: "There's my little lobster." Don't you remember how you wanted to put out the light and how you loved me in the dark? I thought that was nice and respectful. Don't you remember?

FRED : No.

LIZZIE : And when we pretended we were two babies in the same crib? Don't you remember that?

FRED : I tell you to shut up. What's done at night belongs to the night. In the daytime you don't talk about it.

LIZZIE : And if it gives me a kick to talk about it? I had a good time, you know.

FRED : Sure, you had a good time! [*He approaches her, gently kisses her shoulders, then takes her by the throat.*] You always enjoy yourself when you've got a man wrapped up. [*A pause.*] I've forgotten all about it, your wonderful night. Completely forgotten it. I remember the dance hall, that's all. If there was anything else, you're the only one who remembers it. [*He presses his hands to her throat.*]

LIZZIE : What are you doing?

FRED : Just holding your throat in my hands.

LIZZIE : You're hurting me.

FRED : You are the only one who remembers. If I were to squeeze a tiny bit harder, there would be no one in the world to remember last night. [*He releases her.*] How much do you want?

LIZZIE : If you don't remember, it must be because I didn't do my work well. I wouldn't charge for a bad job.

FRED : Cut the comedy. How much?

LIZZIE : Look here; I've been in this place since the day before yesterday. You were the first one to visit me. The first customer gets me free; it brings luck.

FRED : I don't need your presents. [*He puts a ten-dollar bill on the table.*]

LIZZIE : I don't want your dough, but I'd like to know how much you think I'm worth. Wait, let me guess! [*She picks up the bill with her eyes closed.*] Forty dollars? No, that's too much, and anyway there would be two bills. Twenty dollars? No? Then this must be more than forty dollars. Fifty. A hundred? [*All the while,* FRED *watches her, laughing silently.*] I hate to do this, but I'm going to look. [*She looks at the bill.*] Haven't you made a mistake?

FRED : I don't think so.

LIZZIE : You know what you gave me?

FRED : Yes.

LIZZIE : Take it back. Take it right back. [*He makes a gesture of refusal.*] Ten dollars! Ten dollars! That's what I call a good lay—a young girl like me for ten dollars? Did you see my legs? [*She shows him her legs.*] And my breasts? Did you see them? Are these ten-dollar breasts? Take your ten bucks and scram, before I get sore. Ten bucks! My lord kisses me all over, my lord keeps wanting to start all over again, my lord asks me to tell him about my childhood, and this morning my lord thinks he can crab, and complain, as if he paid me by the month; and all for how much? Not for forty, not for thirty, not for twenty: for ten dollars!

FRED : For pigging around, that's a lot.

LIZZIE: Pig yourself. Where do you come from, you hayseed? Your mother must have been a fine slut if she didn't teach you to respect women.

FRED: Will you shut up?

LIZZIE: A fine bitch! A fine bitch!

FRED [*with cold rage*]: My advice to you, young women, is don't talk to the fellows around here about their mothers, if you don't want to get your neck twisted.

LIZZIE [*approaching him*]: Go on, strangle me! Strangle me! Let's see you do it!

FRED [*retreating*]: Don't get excited. [LIZZIE *takes a vase from the table, with the evident intention of throwing it at him.*] Here's ten dollars more, just don't get excited. Don't get excited or I'll have you run in.

LIZZIE: You, you're going to have me run in?

FRED: Yes. Me.

LIZZIE: You?

FRED: Me.

LIZZIE: That I'd like to see!

FRED: I'm Clarke's son.

LIZZIE: Which Clarke?

FRED: Senator Clarke.

LIZZIE: Yeah? And I'm Roosevelt's daughter.

FRED: Have you ever seen a picture of Senator Clarke in the papers?

LIZZIE: Yeah. So what?

FRED: Here it is. [*He shows her a photograph.*] I'm there next to him. He's got his arm around my shoulder.

LIZZIE [*suddenly calm*] : Look at that! Gosh, he's a good-looking man, your father. Let me see. [FRED *snatches the photograph out of her hands.*]

FRED : That's enough.

LIZZIE : He looks so nice—sorta kind and yet firm! Is it true that he's got a silver tongue? [*He doesn't answer.*] Is this your garden?

FRED : Yes.

LIZZIE : He looks so tall. And those little girls on the chairs—are they your sisters? [*He doesn't reply.*] Is your house on the hill?

FRED : Yes.

LIZZIE : Then, when you get your breakfast in the morning, you can see the whole town from your window?

FRED : Yes.

LIZZIE : Do they ring a bell at mealtime to call you? You might answer me.

FRED : We have a gong for that.

LIZZIE [*in ecstasy*] : A gong! I don't understand you. With such a family and such a house, you'd have to pay me to sleep out. [*A pause.*] I'm sorry I said that about your mother; I was mad. Is she in the picture too?

FRED : I've forbidden you to talk about her.

LIZZIE : All right, all right. [*A pause.*] Can I ask you a question? [*He doesn't answer.*] If it disgusts you to make love, why did you come here to me? [*He doesn't answer. She sighs.*] Well, as long as I'm here, I guess I'll have to get used to your ways.

[*A pause.* FRED *combs his hair in front of the mirror.*]

FRED : You're from up North?

LIZZIE : Yes.

FRED : From New York?

LIZZIE : What's it to you?

FRED : You spoke of New York, just before.

LIZZIE : Anyone can talk about New York. That doesn't prove a thing.

FRED : Why didn't you stay up there?

LIZZIE : I was fed up.

FRED : Trouble?

LIZZIE : Yes, sure. I attract trouble; some people are like that. You see this snake? [*She shows him her bracelet.*] It brings bad luck.

FRED : Why do you wear it?

LIZZIE : As long as I have it, I have to keep it. It's supposed to be pretty awful—a snake's revenge.

FRED : You were the one the nigger tried to rape?

LIZZIE : What's that?

FRED : You arrived the day before yesterday, on the six-o'clock express?

LIZZIE : Yes.

FRED : Then you must be the one.

LIZZIE : No one tried to rape me. [*She laughs, not without a trace of bitterness.*] Rape me! That's a good one!

FRED : It's you; Webster told me yesterday, on the dance floor.

LIZZIE : Webster? [*A pause.*] So that's it!

FRED : That's what?

LIZZIE : So that's what made your eyes shine. It excited you, huh? You bastard! With such a good father.

FRED : You little fool! [*A pause.*] If I thought you had slept with a nigger—

LIZZIE : Go on.

FRED : I have five colored servants. When they call me to the phone, they wipe it off before they hand it to me.

LIZZIE [*whistles admiringly*] : I see.

FRED [*calmly*] : We don't like niggers too much here, and we don't like white folk who play around with them.

LIZZIE : That'll do. I have nothing against them, but I don't like them to touch me.

FRED : How could anyone be sure? You are the Devil. The nigger is the Devil too. [*Abruptly*] So he tried to rape you?

LIZZIE : What's it to you?

FRED : The two of them came over to your seat. Then after a while they jumped on you. You called for help and some white people came. One of the niggers flashed his razor, and a white man shot him. The other nigger got away.

LIZZIE : Is that what Webster told you?

FRED : Yes.

LIZZIE : Where did he get that story?

FRED : It's all over town.

LIZZIE : All over town? That's just my luck. Haven't you got anything else to talk about?

FRED : Did it happen the way I said?

LIZZIE : Not at all. The two niggers kept to themselves and didn't even look at me. Then four white men got on the train, and two of them made passes at me. They had just won a football game, and they were drunk. They said that they could smell nigger and wanted to throw them out of the window. The blacks fought back as well as they could, and one of the white men got punched in the eye. And that was when he pulled out a gun and fired. That was all. The other nigger jumped off the train as we were coming into the station.

FRED : We know who it is. He'll gain nothing by waiting. [*A pause.*] When you come up before the judge, are you going to tell him the story you just told me?

LIZZIE : What's it to you?

FRED : Answer me.

LIZZIE : I am not coming up before any judge. I told you I hate any trouble.

FRED : You'll have to appear in court.

LIZZIE : I won't go. I don't want anything more to do with the cops.

FRED : They'll come and get you.

LIZZIE : Then I'll tell them what I saw. [*A pause.*]

FRED : Do you realize what that means?

LIZZIE : What does that mean?

FRED : It means testifying against a white man in behalf of a nigger.

LIZZIE : But suppose the white man is guilty.

FRED : He isn't guilty.

LIZZIE : Since he killed, he's guilty.

◇◇

FRED : Guilty of what?

LIZZIE : Of killing!

FRED : But it was a nigger he killed.

LIZZIE : So what?

FRED : If you were guilty every time you killed a nigger—

LIZZIE : He had no right.

FRED : What right?

LIZZIE : He had no right.

FRED : That right comes from up North. [*A pause.*] Guilty or not, you can't punish a fellow of your own race.

LIZZIE : I don't want to have anyone punished. They'll just ask me what I saw, and I'll tell them. [*A pause.* FRED *comes up to her.*]

FRED : What is there between you and this nigger? Why are you protecting him?

LIZZIE : I don't even know him.

FRED : Then what's the trouble?

LIZZIE : I just want to tell the truth.

FRED : The truth! A ten-dollar whore who wants to tell the truth! There is no truth; there's only whites and blacks, that's all. Seventeen thousand white men, twenty thousand niggers. This isn't New York; we can't fool around down here. [*A pause.*] Thomas is my cousin.

LIZZIE : What?

FRED : Thomas, the one who killed the nigger; he's my cousin.

LIZZIE [*surprised*] : Oh!

FRED : He comes from a good family. That might not

mean much to you, but he's from a good family all the same.

LIZZIE : Good! A guy who kept rubbing up against me and tried to put his hand under my skirt. I can do without such gentlemen. I'm not surprised that you both come from the same family.

FRED [*raising his hand*] : You dirty bitch! [*He controls himself.*] You are the Devil, and with the Devil you can't win. He put his hand under your skirt, he shot down a dirty nigger; so what? You do things like that without thinking; they don't count. Thomas is a leading citizen, that's what counts.

LIZZIE : Maybe so. But the nigger didn't do anything.

FRED : A nigger has always done something.

LIZZIE : I'd never rat on anyone.

FRED : If it's not on him, it'll be on Thomas. You'll have to give away one of them, whatever you do. You'll just have to choose.

LIZZIE : So there we are! Here's me in it up to my neck—just for a change. [*To her bracelet*] God damn you, can't you pick on anyone else? [*She throws the bracelet on the floor.*]

FRED : How much do you want?

LIZZIE : I don't want a cent.

FRED : Five hundred dollars.

LIZZIE : Not a cent.

FRED : It would take you much more than one night to earn five hundred dollars.

LIZZIE : Especially if all I get is tightwads like you. [*A pause.*] So that's why you picked me up last night?

◇◇

FRED : Oh, hell.

LIZZIE : So that was why. You said to yourself: "There's the babe. I'll go home with her and arrange the whole thing." So that's what you wanted! You tickled my hand, but you were as cold as ice. You were thinking: "How'll I get her to do it?" [*A pause.*] But tell me this! Tell me this, my boy. If you came up here with me to talk business, did you have to sleep with me? Huh? Why did you sleep with me, you bastard? Why did you sleep with me?

FRED : Damned if I know.

LIZZIE [*sinks into a chair, weeping*] : Oh, you dirty, filthy bastard!

FRED : Five hundred dollars. Don't cry, for Christ's sake! Five hundred dollars! Stop bawling! Stop bawling! Look, Lizzie! Lizzie! Be reasonable! Five hundred dollars!

LIZZIE [*sobbing*] : I'm not reasonable, and I don't want your five hundred dollars. I just don't want to bear false witness. I want to go back to New York, I want to get out of here! I want to get out of here! [*The bell rings. Startled, she stops crying. The bell rings again. Whispering*] Who is it? Be quiet. [*A long ring.*] I won't open. Be still. [*Knocking on the door.*]

A VOICE : Open up. Police.

LIZZIE [*in a low voice*] : The cops. I knew it had to happen. [*She exhibits the bracelet.*] It's this thing's fault. [*She kisses it and puts it back on her arm.*] I guess I'd better keep it on me. Hide. [*Knocking on the door.*]

THE VOICE : Police!

LIZZIE : But why don't you go hide? Go in the toilet. [*He doesn't budge. She pushes him with all her strength.*] Well, go on! Get out!

THE VOICE : Are you there, Fred? Fred? Are you there?

FRED : Yes, I'm here. [*He brushes her aside. She looks at him with amazement.*]

LIZZIE : So that's what you were after!

[FRED *opens the door and admits* JOHN *and* JAMES. *The door to the street remains open.*]

JOHN : Police. Are you Lizzie MacKay?

LIZZIE [*without hearing him, continues to look at* FRED] : So that's why!

JOHN [*shaking her by the shoulder*] : Answer when you are spoken to.

LIZZIE : What? Yes, that's me.

JOHN : Your papers.

LIZZIE [*makes an effort to control herself*] : What right have you got to question me? What are you doing in my place? [JOHN *shows his badge.*] Anyone can wear a star. You're buddies of my fine gentleman here and you're ganging up on me to make me talk.

JOHN [*showing his police card*] : You know what that is?

LIZZIE [*indicating* JAMES] : How about him?

JOHN [*to* JAMES] : Show her your card.

[JAMES *shows it to her.* LIZZIE *looks at it, goes to the table, without saying anything, pulls out some papers, and gives them to the men.*]

JOHN [*pointing to* FRED] : You brought him here last night, right? You know that prostitution is against the law?

LIZZIE : Are you sure you can come in here without a warrant? Aren't you afraid I'll make trouble for you?

JOHN : Don't you worry about us. [*A pause.*] I asked if you brought him up here to your place?

LIZZIE [*since the police entered she has changed; she has become more hard and vulgar*] : Don't crack your skull. Sure, I brought him up to my place. I let him have it for free. That burns you up, doesn't it?

FRED : You will find two ten-dollar bills on the table. They are mine.

LIZZIE : Prove it!

FRED [*to the two others, without looking at her*] : I picked them up at the bank yesterday morning with twenty-eight others of the same series. You've only got to check up on the serial numbers.

LIZZIE [*violently*] : I wouldn't take them. I refused his filthy money. I threw it in his face.

JOHN : If you refused, why is it lying on the table?

LIZZIE [*after a pause*] : That does it. [*She looks at* FRED *in a kind of stupor and says, almost tenderly*] : So that's what you were up to? [*To the others*] Well, what do you want?

JOHN : Sit down. [*To* FRED] You told her what's what? [FRED *nods.*] I told you to sit down. [*He pushes her into a chair.*] The judge agrees to let Thomas go if he has a signed statement from you. The statement has already been written for you; all you have to do is sign it. Tomorrow there'll be a formal hearing. Can you read? [LIZZIE *shrugs her shoulders, and he hands her a paper.*] Read it and sign.

LIZZIE : Lies from beginning to end.

JOHN : Maybe so. So what?

LIZZIE : I won't sign.

FRED : Take her along. [*To* LIZZIE] It's eighteen months, you know.

LIZZIE : Eighteen months, yes. But when I get out, I'll fry your hide.

FRED : Not if I can help it. [*They look at each other.*] You might telegraph New York; I think she's wanted up there for something.

LIZZIE [*admiringly*] : You're as bitchy as a woman. I never thought I'd meet a guy who could be such a bastard.

JOHN : Make up your mind. Either you sign or it's the cooler.

LIZZIE : I prefer the cooler. I don't want to lie.

FRED : Not lie, you slut! And what did you do all night? When you called me "honey baby," "lover man," I suppose you weren't lying. When you sighed to make me think I was giving you a thrill, weren't you lying?

LIZZIE [*defiantly*] : You'd like to think so, wouldn't you? No, I wasn't lying. [*They stare at each other. FRED looks away.*]

FRED : Let's get this over with. Here's my fountain pen. Sign.

LIZZIE : You can put it away.

[*A pause. The three men seem embarrassed.*]

FRED : So that's the way it is! The finest fellow in town, and his life depends on the whim of a floozy like this! [*He walks up and down, then comes abruptly up to* LIZZIE.] Look at him. [*He shows her a photograph.*] You've seen a man or two, in your filthy trade. Have you ever seen a face like that? Look at that forehead, look at that chin, look at the medals on his uniform. No, no, don't look away. There is no getting out of it: here's your victim, you have got to face him. See how young he is, how straight he stands. Isn't he handsome? But don't you worry, when he leaves prison, ten years from now, he will be bent like an old man, bald and toothless. But you'll be proud of your good work. You were just a little chiseler until now; but this time, you're dealing with a real man, and you want to take his life. What do you say to that? Are you rotten to the core? [*He forces her to her knees.*] On your knees, whore. On your knees before the picture of the man you want to dishonor! [CLARKE *enters through the door they have left open.*]

THE SENATOR : Let her go. [*To* LIZZIE] Get up.

FRED : Hello!

JOHN : Hello!

THE SENATOR : Hello! Hello!

JOHN [*to* LIZZIE] : Meet Senator Clarke.

THE SENATOR [*to* LIZZIE] : Hello!

LIZZIE : Hello!

THE SENATOR : Fine! Now we've all been introduced. [*He looks at* LIZZIE.] So this is the young lady. She impresses me as a mighty nice girl.

FRED : She doesn't want to sign.

THE SENATOR : She is perfectly right. You break in on her without having the right to do so. [*Then, more, forcefully, to forestall* JOHN] Without having the slightest right to do so. You are brutal to her, and you try to make her go against her own conscience. This is not the American way. Did the Negro rape you, my child?

LIZZIE : No.

THE SENATOR : Excellent. So that is clear. Look me in the eyes. [*He looks at her fixedly.*] I am sure she is telling the truth. [*A pause.*] Poor Mary! [*To the others*] Well, boys, let's go. There is nothing more to be done here. Let's make our apologies to the young lady and go.

LIZZIE : Who's Mary?

THE SENATOR : Mary? She is my sister, the mother of this unfortunate Thomas. A poor, dear old lady, who is going to be killed by all this. Good-by, my child.

LIZZIE [*in a choking voice*] : Senator!

THE SENATOR : My child?

LIZZIE : I'm sorry.

THE SENATOR : Why should you be sorry, when you have told the truth?

LIZZIE : I am sorry that—that that's the truth.

THE SENATOR : There is nothing either of us can do about that. And no one has the right to ask you to bear false witness. [*A pause.*] No. Don't think of her any more.

LIZZIE : Who?

THE SENATOR : Of my sister. Weren't you thinking about my sister?

LIZZIE : Yes.

THE SENATOR : I can read your mind, my child. Do you want me to tell you what's going on in your head? [*Imitating* LIZZIE] "If I signed, the Senator would go to her and say: 'Lizzie MacKay is a good girl, and she's the one who's giving your son back to you.' And she would smile through her tears. She would say: 'Lizzie MacKay? I shall not forget that name.' And I who have no family, relegated by cruel fate to social banishment, I would know that a dear little old lady was thinking of me in her great house; that an American mother had taken me to her heart." Poor Lizzie, think no more about it.

LIZZIE : Has she white hair?

THE SENATOR : Completely white. But her face has stayed young. And if you could see her smile— She'll never smile again. Good-by. Tomorrow you shall tell the judge the truth.

LIZZIE : Are you going?

THE SENATOR : Why, yes; I am going to her house. I shall have to tell her about our conversation.

LIZZIE : She knows you are here?

THE SENATOR : She begged me to come to you.

LIZZIE : My God! And she's waiting? And you're going to tell her that I refused to sign. How she will hate me!

THE SENATOR [*putting his hands on her shoulders*] : My poor child, I wouldn't want to be in your shoes.

LIZZIE : What a mess! [*Addressing her bracelet*] It's all your fault, you filthy thing.

THE SENATOR : What?

LIZZIE : Nothing. [*A pause.*] As things stand, it's too bad the nigger didn't really rape me.

THE SENATOR [*touched*] : My child.

LIZZIE [*sadly*] : It would have meant so much to you, and it would have been so little trouble for me.

THE SENATOR : Thank you. [*A pause.*] I should so like to help you. [*A pause.*] Alas, the truth is the truth.

LIZZIE [*sadly*] : Yeah, sure.

THE SENATOR : And the truth is that the Negro didn't rape you.

LIZZIE [*sadly still*] : Yeah, sure.

THE SENATOR : Yes. [*A pause.*] Of course, here we have a truth of the first degree.

LIZZIE [*not understanding*] : Of the first degree.

THE SENATOR : Yes. I mean—a common truth.

LIZZIE : Common? Isn't that the truth?

THE SENATOR : Yes, yes, it is the truth. It's just that— there are various kinds of truths.

LIZZIE : You think the nigger raped me?

THE SENATOR : No. No, he didn't rape you. From a certain point of view, he didn't rape you at all. But, you see, I am an old man, who has lived a long time, who has made many mistakes, but for some time now I have been a little less often mistaken. And my opinion about this is utterly different from yours.

LIZZIE : What opinion?

THE SENATOR : How can I explain it to you? Look:

suppose Uncle Sam suddenly stood before you. What would he say?

LIZZIE [*frightened*] : I don't suppose he would have much of anything to say to me.

THE SENATOR : Are you a Communist?

LIZZIE : Good Lord, no!

THE SENATOR : Then Uncle Sam would have many things to tell you. He would say: "Lizzie, you have reached a point where you must choose between two of my boys. One of them must go. What can you do in a case like this? Well, you keep the better man. Well, then, let us try to see which is the better one. Will you?"

LIZZIE [*carried away*] : Yes, I want to. Oh, I am sorry, I thought it was you saying all that.

THE SENATOR : I was speaking in his name. [*He goes on, as before.*] "Lizzie, this Negro whom you are protecting, what good is he? Somehow or other he was born, God knows where. I nourished and raised him, and how does he pay me back? What does he do for me? Nothing at all; he dawdles, he chisels, he sings, he buys pink and green suits. He is my son, and I love him as much as I do my other boys. But I ask you: does he live like a man? I would not even notice if he died."

LIZZIE : My, how fine you talk.

THE SENATOR : [*in the same vein*] : "The other one, this Thomas, has killed a Negro, and that's very bad. But I need him. He is a hundred-per-cent American, comes from one of our oldest families, has studied at Harvard, is an officer—I need officers—he employs two

thousand workers in his factory—two thousand un-
employed if he happened to die. He's a leader, a
firm bulwark against the Communists, labor unions,
and the Jews. His duty is to live, and yours is to
preserve his life. That's all. Now, choose."

LIZZIE : My, how well you talk!

THE SENATOR : Choose!

LIZZIE [*startled*] : How's that? Oh yes. [*A pause.*]
You mixed me up, I don't know where I am.

THE SENATOR : Look at me, Lizzie. Do you have confidence in me?

LIZZIE : Yes, Senator.

THE SENATOR : Do you believe that I would urge you to
do anything wrong?

LIZZIE : No, Senator.

THE SENATOR : Then I urge you to sign. Here is my pen.

LIZZIE : You think she'll be pleased with me?

THE SENATOR : Who?

LIZZIE : Your sister.

THE SENATOR : She will love you, from a distance, as her
very own child.

LIZZIE : Perhaps she'll send me some flowers?

THE SENATOR : Very likely.

LIZZIE : Or her picture with an inscription.

THE SENATOR : It's quite possible.

LIZZIE : I'd hang it on the wall. [*A pause. She walks up
and down, much agitated.*] What a mess! [*Coming
up to* THE SENATOR *again*] What will you do to the
nigger if I sign?

THE SENATOR : To the nigger? Pooh! [*He takes her by
the shoulders.*] If you sign, the whole town will

adopt you. The whole town. All the mothers in it.

LIZZIE : But—

THE SENATOR : Do you suppose that a whole town could be mistaken? A whole town, with its ministers and its priests, its doctors, its lawyers, its artists, its mayor and his aides, with all its charities? Do you think that could happen?

LIZZIE : No, no, no.

THE SENATOR : Give me your hand. [*He forces her to sign.*] So now it's done. I thank you in the name of my sister and my nephew, in the name of the seventeen thousand white inhabitants of our town, in the name of the American people, whom I represent in these parts. Give me your forehead, my child. [*He kisses her on the forehead.*] Come along, boys. [*To* LIZZIE] I shall see you later in the evening; we still have something to talk about. [*He goes out.*]

FRED [*leaving*] : Good-by, Lizzie.

LIZZIE : Good-by. [*They all go out. She stands there overwhelmed, then rushes to the door.*] Senator! Senator! I don't want to sign! Tear up the paper! Senator! [*She comes back to the front of the stage and mechanically takes hold of the vacuum cleaner.*] Uncle Sam! [*She turns on the sweeper.*] Something tells me I've been had—but good! [*She pushes the vacuum cleaner furiously.*]

CURTAIN

SCENE TWO

*Same setting, twelve hours later. The lamps are lit, the
windows are open. In the night, a growing clamor
outside.* THE NEGRO *appears at the window, straddles
the window-sill, and jumps into the empty room. He
crosses to the middle of the stage. The bell rings. He
hides behind a curtain.* LIZZIE *emerges from the bathroom, crosses to the street door, and opens it.*

LIZZIE : Come in! [THE SENATOR *enters.*] Well?

THE SENATOR : Thomas is in the arms of his mother. I
have come to bring you their thanks.

LIZZIE : Is she happy?

THE SENATOR : Supremely happy.

LIZZIE : Did she cry?

THE SENATOR : Cry? Why should she cry? She is a
woman of character.

LIZZIE : But you said she would cry.

THE SENATOR : That was just a manner of speaking.

LIZZIE : She didn't expect this, did she? She thought I
was a bad woman and that I would testify for the
nigger.

THE SENATOR : She put her trust in God.

LIZZIE : What does she think of me?

THE SENATOR : She thanks you.

LIZZIE : Didn't she ask what I looked like?

THE SENATOR : No.

LIZZIE : She thinks I'm a good girl?

◇◇◇

THE SENATOR : She thinks you did your duty.

LIZZIE : She does?

THE SENATOR : She hopes that you will continue to do it.

LIZZIE : Oh yes, yes.

THE SENATOR : Lizzie, look me in the eyes. [*He takes her by the shoulders.*] You will continue to do your duty? You aren't going to disappoint her?

LIZZIE : Don't you worry. I can't go back on what I said; they'd throw me in the clink. [*A pause.*] What's all that shouting about?

THE SENATOR : Pay no attention.

LIZZIE : I can't stand it any more. [*She closes the window.*] Senator?

THE SENATOR : My child?

LIZZIE : You are sure that we haven't made a mistake, that I really did what I should?

THE SENATOR : Absolutely sure.

LIZZIE : I don't know where I am any more; you've mixed me up; you're too quick for me. What time is it?

THE SENATOR : Eleven o'clock.

LIZZIE : Eight hours left until daylight. I know I won't be able to sleep a wink. [*A pause.*] It's just as hot at night here as when the sun is up. [*A pause.*] What about the nigger?

THE SENATOR : What Negro? Oh, yes, of course, they are looking for him.

LIZZIE : What will they do to him? [THE SENATOR *shrugs his shoulders. The shouting outside increases.* LIZZIE *goes to the window.*] What is all this shouting for? Men are running about with flashlights and dogs. Are they celebrating something? Or— Tell me what's up, Senator! Tell me what's going on!

THE SENATOR [*taking a letter out of his pocket*] : My sister asked me to give you this.

LIZZIE [*with interest*] : She's written me? [*She tears open the envelope, and takes from it a hundred-dollar bill, rummages in it to find a letter, finds none, crushes the envelope, and throws it on the floor. She takes a different tone now.*] A hundred dollars. You've done very well; your son promised me five hundred. You got a bargain.

THE SENATOR : My child.

LIZZIE : You can thank the lady. You can tell her that I'd rather've had a porcelain vase or some nylons, something she took the trouble to pick out for me herself. But it's the intention that counts, isn't it? [*A pause.*] You've had me good. [*They face each other.* THE SENATOR *moves closer to her.*]

THE SENATOR : I thank you, my child; we'll have a little talk—just the two of us. You're facing a moral crisis and need my help.

LIZZIE : What I particularly need is some dough, but I think we can make a deal, you and me. [*A pause.*] Until now I liked old men best, because they looked so respectable, but I'm beginning to wonder if they're not more crooked than the others.

THE SENATOR [*gaily*] : Crooked! I wish my colleagues could hear you. What wonderful frankness! There is something in you that your deplorable circumstances have not spoiled! [*He pats her.*] Yes indeed. Something. [*She submits to him, passive but scornful.*] I'll be back, don't bother to see me out.

[*He goes out.* LIZZIE *is immobile, as if paralyzed. She picks up the bill, crumples it, throws it on the floor, falls into a chair, and bursts into sobs. Outside, the yelling is closer and more intense. Pistol-shots in the distance.* THE NEGRO *emerges from his hiding-place. He plants himself in front of her. She raises her head and gives a startled cry.*]

LIZZIE : Ah! [*A pause. She rises.*] I knew you'd show up. I just knew it. How did you get in?

THE NEGRO : Through the window.

LIZZIE : What do you want?

THE NEGRO : Hide me.

LIZZIE : I told you, no.

THE NEGRO : You hear them out there, ma'am?

LIZZIE : Yes.

THE NEGRO : That's the beginning of the hunt.

LIZZIE : What hunt?

THE NEGRO : The nigger hunt.

LIZZIE : Oh! [*A long pause.*] Are you sure no one saw you come in?

THE NEGRO : Yes, I'm sure.

LIZZIE : What will they do to you if they get you?

THE NEGRO : Gasoline.

LIZZIE : What?

THE NEGRO : Gasoline. [*He makes an expressive gesture.*] They'll set me on fire.

LIZZIE : I see. [*She goes to the window and draws the curtain.*] Sit down. [THE NEGRO *falls into a chair.*]

You just had to come here! Won't I ever get out of this? [*She approaches him almost threateningly.*] I hate trouble, don't you understand? [*Tapping her foot.*] I hate it! I hate it! I hate it!

THE NEGRO: They think I harmed you, ma'am.

LIZZIE: So what?

THE NEGRO: So they won't look for me here.

LIZZIE: Do you know why they are after you?

THE NEGRO: Because they suppose I wronged you, ma'am.

LIZZIE: Do you know who told them that?

THE NEGRO: No.

LIZZIE: I did. [*A long silence.* THE NEGRO *looks at her.*] What do you think of that?

THE NEGRO: Why did you do that, ma'am? Oh, why did you do that?

LIZZIE: That's what I keep asking myself.

THE NEGRO: They won't have any pity; they'll whip me across the eyes, they'll pour their cans of gas over me. Oh, why did you do it? I didn't harm you.

LIZZIE: Oh yes, you did too. You can't imagine how much you've harmed me. [*A pause.*] Don't you want to choke me?

THE NEGRO: Lots of times they force people to say things they don't mean.

LIZZIE: Yes, lots of times. And when they can't force them, they mix them up with their sweet talk. [*A pause.*] Well? No? You're not going to choke me? You're a good guy. [*A pause.*] I'll hide you until to-morrow night. [*He makes a move.*] Don't touch me; I don't like niggers. [*Shouts and pistol-shots out-*

side.] They're getting closer. [*She goes to the window, draws the curtains, and looks out into the street.*] We're cooked.

THE NEGRO : What are they doing?

LIZZIE : They've put guards at both ends of the block, and they are searching all the houses. You just had to come here. Someone must have seen you come down the street. [*She looks out again.*] This is it. It's our turn. They are coming up here.

THE NEGRO : How many?

LIZZIE : Five or six. The others are waiting outside. [*She turns toward him again.*] Don't shake so. Good God, don't shake so! [*A pause. To her bracelet*] It's all your fault! You pig of a snake! [*She tears it from her arm, throws it on the floor, and tramples on it.*] Trash! [*To* THE NEGRO] You just had to come here. [THE NEGRO *rises, as if about to leave.*] Stay put. If you go out you're done for.

THE NEGRO : What about the roof?

LIZZIE : With this moon? You can go on up if you feel like being a target. [*A pause.*] Wait a second. They have two floors to search before ours. I told you not to shake so. [*A long silence. She walks up and down.* THE NEGRO, *completely overcome, stays in the chair.*] Do you have a gun?

THE NEGRO : Oh, no!

LIZZIE : All right. [*She rummages in a drawer and brings out a revolver.*]

THE NEGRO : What's that for, ma'am?

LIZZIE : I am going to open the door and ask them to come in. For twenty-five years I have had to take their crap about old mothers with white hair, about war heroes, about Uncle Sam. But now I've caught on. They won't get away with it altogether. I'll open the door and say to them: "He's inside. He's here, but he's done nothing; I was forced to sign a false statement. I swear by Christ that he did nothing."

THE NEGRO : They won't believe you.

LIZZIE : Maybe not. Maybe they won't believe me; but then you'll cover them with the gun, and if they still come after you, you can shoot.

THE NEGRO : Others will come.

LIZZIE : Shoot them too! And if you see the Senator's son, try not to miss him; he's the one who cooked this whole thing up. We're cornered, aren't we? Anyhow, this is our last chance 'cause if they find you here with me I won't be worth a plugged nickel. So we might as well kick off in company. [*She offers him the revolver.*] Take it! I tell you to take it!

THE NEGRO : I can't, ma'am.

LIZZIE : Why not?

THE NEGRO : I can't shoot white folks.

LIZZIE : Really! That would bother them, wouldn't it?

THE NEGRO : They're white folks, ma'am.

LIZZIE : So what? Maybe they got a right to bleed you like a pig just because they're white?

THE NEGRO : But they're white folks.

LIZZIE : What a laugh! You know, you're like me; you're just as big a sucker as I am. Still, when they all get together—

THE NEGRO : Why don't you shoot, ma'am?

LIZZIE : I told you that I'm a sucker. [*There are steps on*

the stairway.] Here they come. [*A sharp laugh.*]
We're sure sitting pretty. [*A pause.*] Get in the toilet
and don't budge. Hold your breath.

[THE NEGRO *obeys.* LIZZIE *waits. The bell rings. She
crosses herself, picks up the bracelet, and goes to open
the door. There are men with guns.*]

FIRST MAN : We're looking for the nigger.

LIZZIE : What nigger?

FIRST MAN : The one that raped the woman in the train
and cut the Senator's nephew with a razor.

LIZZIE : Well, by God, you won't find him here! [*A
pause.*] Don't you recognize me?

SECOND MAN : Yes, yes. I saw you get off the train the
day before yesterday.

LIZZIE : That's right. Because I'm the one who was
raped, you understand? [*Exclamations. They look
at her with fascination, desire, and a kind of horror.
They draw back a little.*] If he messes around here,
he'll get a little of this. [*She flourishes the revolver.
They laugh.*]

FIRST MAN : Don't you want to see him lynched?

LIZZIE : Come for me when you get him.

FIRST MAN : That won't be long, sugar; we know he's
hiding in this block.

LIZZIE : Good luck. [*They go out. She shuts the door
and puts the revolver on the table.*] You can come
out. [THE NEGRO *emerges, kneels, and kisses the hem
of her skirt.*] I told you not to touch me. [*She looks
him over.*] Just the same, you must be a queer character, to have a whole town after you.

THE NEGRO: I didn't do anything, ma'am, you know I didn't do anything.

LIZZIE: They say a nigger's always done something.

THE NEGRO: Never did anything. Never, never.

LIZZIE [*wiping her brow with her hand*]: I don't know what's right any more. [*A pause.*] Just the same, a whole city can't be completely wrong. [*A pause.*] Oh, shit! I don't understand anything any more.

THE NEGRO: That's how it goes, ma'am. That's how it always goes with white folks.

LIZZIE: You too? You feel guilty?

THE NEGRO: Yes, ma'am.

LIZZIE: But you didn't do anything?

THE NEGRO: No, ma'am.

LIZZIE: What have they got anyhow, that everybody's on their side all the time?

THE NEGRO: They're white folks.

LIZZIE: I'm white too. [*A pause. Sound of steps outside.*] They're coming down again. [*Instinctively she steps closer to him. He trembles, but puts his arm around her shoulders. The sound of steps is fainter. Silence. She suddenly frees herself from his embrace.*] Well, look at us, now! Aren't we alone in the world? Like two orphans. [*The bell rings. They make no answer. The bell rings again.*] Get in the toilet.

[*There is a rapping on the front door.* THE NEGRO *hides.* LIZZIE *goes to open the door. Enter* FRED.]

LIZZIE: Are you crazy? Why come to my door? No, you can't come in, you've given me enough trouble.

Get out, get out, you bastard, get out! Get the hell
out of here! [*He pushes her aside, closes the door,
and takes her by the shoulder. A long pause.*] Well?

FRED : You are the Devil!

LIZZIE : And so you try to break down my door just to
tell me that? What a mess! Where have you been?
[*A pause.*] Answer me.

FRED : They caught a nigger. It wasn't the right one.
But they lynched him just the same.

LIZZIE : So?

FRED : I was with them.

LIZZIE [*whistles*] : I see. [*A pause.*] It begins to look
as if seeing a nigger lynched does something to you.

FRED : I want you.

LIZZIE : What?

FRED : You are the Devil. You've bewitched me. I was
with them, I had my revolver in my hand, and the
nigger was swinging from a branch. I looked at him,
and I thought: "I want her." It's not natural.

LIZZIE : Let go of me! I tell you let go of me.

FRED : What have you done to me, what have you got,
you witch? I looked at the nigger and I saw you. I
saw you swaying above the flames. I fired.

LIZZIE : You filthy bastard! Let me go, let me go. You're
a murderer!

FRED : What have you done to me. You stick to me like
the teeth in my gums. I see your belly, your dirty
whorish belly, I feel your heat in my hands, your
smell in my nostrils. I came running here, and I didn't
even know whether I wanted to kill you or rape you.
Now I know. [*He releases her abruptly.*] I am not

going to damn my soul to hell for a whore. [*He comes
up to her again.*] Was it true what you told me this
morning?

LIZZIE : What?

FRED : That I gave you a thrill?

LIZZIE : Let me alone.

FRED : Swear that it's true. Swear it! [*He twists her
wrist. There is a noise of someone moving in the bathroom.*] What's that? [*He listens.*] Someone's in
there.

LIZZIE : You're out of your mind. There's nobody.

FRED : Yes, in the toilet. [*He goes toward the bathroom.*]

LIZZIE : You can't go in.

FRED : You see, there is someone.

LIZZIE : It's today's customer. A guy who pays. There.
Are you satisfied?

FRED : A customer? No more customers for you. Never
any more. You belong to me. [*A pause.*] I must see
what he looks like. [*He shouts*] Come out of there!

LIZZIE [*shouting*] : Don't come out. It's a trap.

FRED : You filthy little whore! [*He shoves her out of
the way, goes toward the door, and opens it.* THE
NEGRO *comes out.*] So that's your customer?

LIZZIE : I hid him because they wanted to hurt him.
Don't shoot; you know very well that he's innocent.
[FRED *draws his revolver.* THE NEGRO *gets set, pushes*
FRED *out of the way, and dashes out.* FRED *runs after
him.* LIZZIE *runs to the door, through which the two
men have disappeared, and begins to shout.*]

LIZZIE : He's innocent! He's innocent! [*Two pistol-*

*shots. She comes back into the room, her face hard.
She goes to the table and takes the gun.* FRED *comes
back. She turns toward him, her back to the audience,
holding her gun behind her back.* FRED *puts his gun
on the table.*] So you got him? [FRED *doesn't answer.*] Well, now it's your turn. [*She covers him
with the revolver.*]

FRED : Lizzie! I have a mother!

LIZZIE : Shut your face! They pulled that on me before.

FRED [*approaching her slowly*] : The first Clarke
cleared a whole forest, just by himself; he killed
seventeen Indians with his bare hands before dying
in an ambush; his son practically built this town; he
was friends with George Washington, and died at
Yorktown, for American independence; my great-
grandfather was chief of the Vigilantes in San Fran-
cisco, he saved the lives of twenty-two persons in
the great fire; my grandfather came back to settle
down here, he dug the Mississippi Canal, and was
elected Governor. My father is a Senator. I shall be
senator after him. I am the last one to carry the family name. We have made this country, and its history
is ours. There have been Clarkes in Alaska, in the
Philippines, in New Mexico. Can you dare to shoot
all of America?

LIZZIE : You come closer, and I'll let you have it.

FRED : Go ahead! Shoot! You see, you can't. A girl like
you *can't* shoot a man like me. Who are you? What
do you do in this world? Do you even know who
your grandfather was? I have a right to live; there are

things to be done, and I am expected to do them. Give me the revolver. [*She gives him the revolver, he puts it in his pocket.*] About the nigger, he was running too fast. I missed him. [*A pause. He puts his arms around her.*] I'll put you in a beautiful house, with a garden, on the hill across the river. You'll walk in the garden, but I forbid you to go out; I am very jealous. I'll come to see you after dark, three times a week—on Tuesday, Thursday, and for the week end. You'll have nigger servants, and more money than you ever dreamed of; but you will have to put up with all my whims, and I'll have plenty! [*She yields a bit to his embrace.*] Is it true that I gave you a thrill? Answer me. Is it true?

LIZZIE [*wearily*] : Yes, it's true.

FRED [*patting her on the cheek*] : Then everything is back to normal again. [*A pause.*] My name is Fred.

CURTAIN

THE VICTORS

(*Morts sans sépulture*)

A PLAY IN FOUR ACTS

◇◇

CHARACTERS IN THE PLAY

FRANÇOIS

SORBIER

CANORIS

LUCIE

HENRI

JEAN

CLOCHET

LANDRIEU

PELLERIN

CORBIER

TROOPERS

Morts sans sépulture (*The Victors*) was first presented at the Théâtre Antoine, Paris, on November 8, 1946.

THE VICTORS

A C T   I

*An attic lighted by a dormer window. A hodge-podge
of all sorts of things: trunks, an old stove, a dress-
maker's dummy.* CANORIS *and* SORBIER *are sitting, one
on a trunk, the other on an old stool.* LUCIE *is sitting
on the stove. All are handcuffed.* FRANÇOIS *paces back
and forth. He is handcuffed too.* HENRI *is stretched
out on the floor, asleep.*

FRANÇOIS: For God's sake, say something, will you?
SORBIER [*raising his head*] : What do you want me to
say?
FRANÇOIS: Anything at all, as long as you make some
noise.
[*A sudden shrill burst of popular music. It is the
radio on the floor below.*]
SORBIER: There's noise for you.
FRANÇOIS: Not that: it's *their* noise. [*He begins pacing
again. Then he stops abruptly.*] Ha!
SORBIER: Now what?
FRANÇOIS: They hear me and they're saying: "There's
the first one of them to lose his nerve."

CANORIS : Well, then, don't lose your nerve. Sit down. Put your hands on your knees, and you wrists won't hurt so much. And be quiet. Try to sleep or think.

FRANÇOIS : What good would that do?

[CANORIS *shrugs his shoulders.* FRANÇOIS *goes on pacing.*]

SORBIER : François!

FRANÇOIS : Well?

SORBIER : Your shoes squeak!

FRANÇOIS : I'm making them squeak on purpose. [*A pause. He plants himself right in front of* SORBIER.] Now what can you be thinking about?

SORBIER [*raising his head*] : Do you want me to tell you?

FRANÇOIS [*looks at him and draws back a little*] : No. Don't tell me.

SORBIER : I was thinking of the little girl who screamed.

LUCIE [*suddenly emerging from her dream world*] : What girl?

SORBIER : The little girl on the farm. I heard her screaming when they took us away. The fire had already reached the staircase.

LUCIE : The girl on the farm? You didn't have to tell us.

SORBIER : There are lots of others who are dead. Women and children. But I didn't hear them die. It's as if that girl were still screaming. I couldn't keep her screams for myself alone.

LUCIE : She was thirteen. Because of us she's dead.

SORBIER : It's because of us that they're all dead.

CANORIS [*to* FRANÇOIS] : You see it was better not to talk.

FRANÇOIS: Why not? We're not going to last long either. In a little while maybe you'll think they were lucky.

SORBIER: They didn't want to die.

FRANÇOIS: And do you suppose that I'm reconciled to it? It wasn't our fault that the job failed.

SORBIER: Yes. It was our fault.

FRANÇOIS: We obeyed orders.

SORBIER: Yes.

FRANÇOIS: They told us: "Climb up there and take the village." We told them: "That's absurd; the Germans will be tipped off in twenty-four hours." They replied: "Go up there anyway and take it." Then we said: "O.K." And off we went. How was it our fault?

SORBIER: We should have succeeded.

FRANÇOIS: We couldn't succeed.

SORBIER: I know. But we should have just the same. [A pause.] Three hundred. Three hundred people who didn't want to die and who died for nothing. They are lying among the stones, and the sun blackens them; they must be visible from every window. Because of us. Because of us, there are only troopers, dead men, and stones in that village. It'll be hard to kick off with those screams in my ears.

FRANÇOIS [shouting]: Leave us alone with your corpses. I'm the youngest: all I did was obey. I am innocent! Innocent! Innocent!

LUCIE [softly; during the whole preceding scene she has remained calm]: François!

FRANÇOIS [abashed, weakly]: What?

LUCIE : Come sit near me, little brother. [*He hesitates. She repeats the command even more gently.*] Come on! [*He sits by her. She awkwardly strokes his face with her bound hands.*] How hot you are! Where is your handkerchief?

FRANÇOIS : In my pocket. I can't get it.

LUCIE : In this pocket?

FRANÇOIS : Yes. [LUCIE *reaches into his coat pocket; laboriously she takes out a handkerchief and wipes his face.*]

LUCIE : You are sweating and shaking; you shouldn't pace so much.

FRANÇOIS : If I could only take off my coat.

LUCIE : Don't think about it, because it's impossible. [*He pulls on his handcuffs.*] No, don't keep hoping to break them. Hope hurts. Be calm, breathe gently, act dead; I'm dead and I'm calm; I'm saving myself.

FRANÇOIS : For what? So as to be able to shriek louder later on? That's like saving candle ends. There is so little time left; I should like to be everywhere at once. [*He is about to get up.*]

LUCIE : Stay here.

FRANÇOIS : I have to keep turning around. When I stop, it's my thoughts that start turning. I don't want to think.

LUCIE : Poor kid.

FRANÇOIS [*lets himself slip to* LUCIE's *knees*] : Lucie, everything is so hard. I can't look at your faces: they frighten me.

LUCIE : Rest your head on my knees. Yes, everything is so hard and you are so young. If only someone could still smile at you and say: "My poor kid." I used to take care of all your troubles. My poor kid—my poor kid. [*She suddenly straightens up.*] I can't any more. Anguish has drained me dry. I can't cry any more.

FRANÇOIS: Don't leave me alone. Ideas come into my head that I'm ashamed of.

LUCIE: Listen. There is *somebody* who can *help you.* I'm not utterly alone. [*A pause.*] Jean is with me, if you could just—

FRANÇOIS: Jean?

LUCIE: They didn't get him. He is on his way to Grenoble. The only one of us who will be alive to-morrow.

FRANÇOIS: So what?

LUCIE: He'll find the others, they'll start all over again somewhere else. And then the war will be over, and they'll live peacefully in Paris, with real photos on real identification cards, and people will call them by their right names.

FRANÇOIS: Well, what of it? He had luck. But what's that to me?

LUCIE: He's going down the hills through the forest. There are poplars below, all along the way. He is thinking of me. There is no one but him in the world who can think of me with that particular sweetness. He's thinking of you too. He thinks you are an unfortunate kid. Try to see yourself with his eyes. He can cry. [*She weeps.*]

FRANÇOIS: You can cry, too.

LUCIE: I'm crying with his tears.

[*A pause.* FRANÇOIS *stands up suddenly.*]

FRANÇOIS : That's enough. I'll end up by hating him.

LUCIE : But you used to love him.

FRANÇOIS : Not the way you loved him.

LUCIE : No. Not the way I loved him.

[*There are steps in the corridor. The door opens.* LUCIE *springs to her feet.* A TROOPER *looks in and then shuts the door.*]

SORBIER [*shrugging his shoulders*] : They're having their fun. Why did you get up?

LUCIE [*sitting down again*] : I thought they had come for us.

CANORIS : They won't come so soon.

LUCIE : Why not?

CANORIS : They're making a mistake: they think waiting is demoralizing.

SORBIER : Is it a mistake? Waiting is no joke when you get ideas.

CANORIS : That's true enough. But on the other hand you have time to collect yourself. My first time was in Greece, under Metaxas. They came to arrest me at four o'clock in the morning. If they had worked on me a bit I would have talked. Out of surprise. But they didn't ask me a thing. Ten days later they tried everything, but it was too late; they had lost the surprise effect.

SORBIER : Did they beat you?

CANORIS : Good God, yes!

SORBIER : With their fists?

CANORIS : With their fists, with their feet.

SORBIER : Did you—want to talk?

CANORIS : No. It's not too bad while they're beating you.

SORBIER : Ah! Not too bad. [*A pause.*] But when they lay into your shins and elbows?

CANORIS : Even then. It's not too bad. [*Gently*] Sorbier.

SORBIER : What?

CANORIS : You mustn't be afraid of them. They have no imagination.

SORBIER : It's myself I'm scared of.

CANORIS : But why? We have nothing to tell them. They know as much as we do. Listen! [*A pause.*] It's not at all like what you imagine it is.

FRANÇOIS : What's it like?

CANORIS : I couldn't tell you. Why, for example, time seemed short to me. [*He laughs.*] My teeth were clenched so tight that for three hours I couldn't open my mouth. This was at Nauplia. There was a guy who wore old-fashioned shoes. With pointed toes. He kicked me in the face. Women were singing outside the window: I remember the tune.

SORBIER : In Nauplia? What year was that?

CANORIS : In '36.

SORBIER : Really? I went through Nauplia that year. I was in Greece on the *Théophile-Gautier*. I took a camping trip. I saw the prison; there were fig trees along the walls. So you were inside and I was outside? [*He laughs.*] That's a riot.

CANORIS : Yeh, it's a riot.

SORBIER [*abruptly*] : But what if they mess around with you?

CANORIS : Huh?

SORBIER : What if they mess around on you with their gadgets? [CANORIS *shrugs his shoulders.*] I suppose I would defend myself out of modesty. Each minute I should say to myself: I'll hold back for just one more minute. Is that a good method?

CANORIS : There is no method.

SORBIER : But what would *you* do?

LUCIE : Can't you be quiet? Look at the kid! Do you think this sort of talk will give him courage? Wait a bit, they'll be glad to teach you.

SORBIER : Leave us alone! Let him put his fingers in his ears if he doesn't want to hear.

LUCIE : And must I hold my ears too? I don't like to hear you because I'm afraid I'll despise you. Do you need all these words to give you courage? I've seen animals die and I should like to die like them: in silence!

SORBIER : Who said anything about dying? We're just talking about what they'll do to us first. You have to get ready for it.

LUCIE : I don't want to get ready for it. Why should I live twice through the hours that lie ahead? Look at Henri: he's sleeping. Why not sleep?

SORBIER : Sleep? And they'll come to shake me and wake me up. No, not for me. I have no time to lose.

LUCIE : Then think of the things you love. I think about Jean, about my life, about the kid when he was sick and I took care of him in a hotel in Arcachon. I could see pine trees and great green waves from my window.

SORBIER [*ironically*] : Green waves, really? I tell you I have no time to lose.

LUCIE : Sorbier, I don't recognize you any more.

SORBIER [*confused*] : All right! Just nerves: I've got the nerves of a virgin. [*He rises and goes toward her.*] Each one defends himself in his own way. I'm no good if you take me by surprise. If I could feel the pain ahead of time—just a little bit, so as to note the transition—I would be surer of myself. It's not my fault; I've always been meticulous. [*A pause.*] I like you a lot, you know that. But I feel that I'm alone. [*A pause.*] If you want me to shut up—

FRANÇOIS : Let them talk. It's the sound they make that counts.

LUCIE : Do as you like.

[*A moment of silence.*]

SORBIER [*in a lowered voice*] : Say, Canoris! [CANORIS *lifts his head.*] Did you ever know anyone who gave in and talked?

CANORIS : Yes, I knew a couple.

SORBIER : And?

CANORIS : What do you care when we've got nothing to tell?

SORBIER : I just wanted to know—could they stand themselves afterwards?

CANORIS : That depends. There was one fellow who shot himself in the face with a shotgun; he only managed to blind himself. I sometimes ran into him in the streets of the Piræus, led by an Armenian. He thought he had paid. Each one decides for himself whether he has paid or not. We knocked off another one at a fair, just as he was buying gumdrops. Since he'd been out of prison he had developed a passion for gumdrops because they're sweet.

SORBIER : The lucky dog.

CANORIS : Hmmmm.

SORBIER : If I squealed I doubt if sweets would console me.

CANORIS : You say that now. But you never can tell before it's happened to you.

SORBIER : Just the same, I don't think I'd like myself much afterwards. I think I'd take down the shotgun.

FRANÇOIS : Me, I prefer the gumdrops.

SORBIER : François!

FRANÇOIS : Why pick on François? Did you warn me when I came looking for you? You told me: the resistance needs men. You didn't tell me it needed heroes. Me, I'm no hero. I'm not a hero! I'm not a hero! I did as I was told: I distributed leaflets and transported arms, and you said I was always cheerful. But nobody took the trouble to let me know what was waiting for me in the end. I swear I never knew what I was getting into.

SORBIER : You knew. You knew that René had been tortured.

FRANÇOIS : I never thought about it. [*A pause.*] You pity the girl who died; you say: it's on account of us that she's dead. But if I should talk when they burn me with their cigars, you would say: he's a coward; and you would hand me a shotgun, if you didn't shoot

me in the back first. And yet I'm only two years
older than she was.

SORBIER : I was just talking for myself.

CANORIS [*going up to* FRANÇOIS] : You have no duty
now, François. Neither duty nor assignment. We
have no information, nothing to keep from them. Let
each one get through it without suffering too much.
The means doesn't matter.

[FRANÇOIS *gradually becomes calmer, but he is exhausted.* LUCIE *presses him to her.*]

SORBIER : The means doesn't matter—of course. Scream,
weep, beg, ask their pardon, dig into your memory to
find something you can confess to, someone to
turn over to them: what of it? There's nothing at
stake; you won't find anything to tell them, all the
little nasty facts will be strictly confidential. Perhaps it is better that way. [*A pause.*] Only I'm not
sure.

CANORIS : What would you like? To know a name or
a date to withhold from them?

SORBIER : I don't know. I don't even know whether I
could keep from talking.

CANORIS : So?

SORBIER : I'd like to know myself. I knew that they'd
get me in the end, and I knew that some day I'd have
my back against the wall, face to face with myself,
without escape. I asked myself if I could face the
music. It's my body that worries me, don't you see?
I have a lousy body, all screwed up with nerves like
a woman. Well, the time has come; they'll go over
me with their gadgets. But I've been robbed: I'm go-

ing to suffer for nothing, I'll die without knowing
what I'm worth.

[*The music stops. They sit up straight, listening.*]

HENRI [*waking up suddenly*] : What's up? [*A pause.*]
The polka is over, it is our turn to dance now, I suppose. [*The music starts up again.*] False alarm. It's
strange how much they like music. [*He gets to his
feet.*] I dreamed that I was dancing, at Scheherazade.
You know Scheherazade, in Paris. I've never been
there. [*He rubs the sleep from his eyes.*] Ah, there
you are—there you are. Do you want to dance,
Lucie?

LUCIE : No.

HENRI : Do your wrists hurt, too? The flesh must have
swollen while I slept. What time is it?

CANORIS : Three o'clock.

LUCIE : Five o'clock.

SORBIER : Six o'clock.

CANORIS : We don't know.

HENRI : You had a watch.

CANORIS : They broke it on my wrist. What we do
know is that you slept a long time.

HENRI : That's time stolen from me. [*To* CANORIS]
Help me up. [CANORIS *gives him a lift, and* HENRI
hoists himself to the window.] It is five o'clock by
the sun. Lucie was right. [*He gets down.*] The town
hall is still burning. So you don't want to dance? [*A
pause.*] I hate that music.

CANORIS [*with indifference*] : Bah!

HENRI : They must be hearing it at the farm.

CANORIS : There is nobody there to hear it now.

HENRI : I know that. But it comes in the window, it whirls over the corpses. Music, the sun, there's a picture for you. And the bodies are all black. Ah! We really missed that one. [*A pause.*] What's wrong with the kid?

LUCIE : He's not feeling well. It's a week since he's had a wink of sleep. What are you made of, to be able to sleep?

HENRI : Sleep came by itself. I felt so alone that it made me sleepy. [*He laughs.*] We are forgotten by the whole world. [*Approaching* FRANÇOIS] Poor kid. [*He strokes his head and turns abruptly to* CANORIS.] What did we do wrong?

CANORIS : I don't know. What good does it do now?

HENRI : Some mistake was made. I feel guilty.

SORBIER : You too? Ah! I'm glad of that. I thought I was the only one.

CANORIS : All right, I feel guilty too. But how does that change anything?

HENRI : I wouldn't want to die guilty.

CANORIS : Take it easy. I'm sure the others won't blame you.

HENRI : To hell with the others. I owe an accounting only to myself now.

CANORIS [*shocked, dryly*] : Well—maybe you want a father confessor?

HENRI : To hell with a priest. I tell you that it's to myself alone that I owe any accounting at this point. [*A pause. As if speaking to himself*] Things shouldn't have gone this way. If I could find the error—

CANORIS : You'd be much better off!

◇◇

HENRI : I could face it squarely and tell myself: this is why I must die. Good God! A man can't die like a rat, for nothing, with not a peep out of him.

CANORIS [*shrugging his shoulders*] : Oh, so what!

SORBIER : Why do you shrug your shoulders? A man has a right to save his death; that's about all he has left.

CANORIS : You're right. Well, let him save it if he can.

HENRI : Thanks for the permission. [*A pause.*] You might just as well start saving your own: we haven't too much time.

CANORIS : My own? Why? Who would it help? It's strictly a personal matter.

HENRI : Strictly personal. Yes. And then what?

CANORIS : I never could interest myself in personal problems. Not other people's nor even my own.

HENRI [*without hearing him*] : If only I could just tell myself that I did what I could. But of course that's asking too much. For thirty years I've felt guilty. Guilty because I was alive. And now, on account of me, houses are burning, innocent people are dead, and I am going to die guilty. My life has been one long mistake. [CANORIS *gets up and goes over to him.*]

CANORIS : You're not modest, Henri.

HENRI : What?

CANORIS : You torment yourself because you're not modest. As far as I'm concerned, we died long ago: at the precise moment we stopped being useful. Right now we have a little bit of posthumous life, a few hours to kill. There's nothing more for you to do except kill time and chat with those around you. Take

it easy, Henri, relax. You have a right to relax now
there's nothing more for us to do here. Relax! We
don't count now; we're dead and of no importance.
[*A pause.*] This is the first time I felt I had the right
to relax.

HENRI: This is the first time in three years that I've
come face to face with myself. I was given orders. I
obeyed them. I felt justified. Now there's nobody to
give me orders and there's nothing that could justify
me. A little bit of excess life—yes. Just enough time
to take stock of myself. [*A pause.*] Canoris, why are
we going to die?

CANORIS: Because we were sent on a dangerous mission
and had no luck.

HENRI: Yes, that's what our comrades will think. That's
what will be said in the official speeches. But I want
to know what *you* think.

CANORIS: I don't think anything. I lived only for the
cause and I always foresaw I would have a death like
this.

HENRI: You lived for the cause, yes. But don't try to
tell me that it's for the cause you are going to die.
Perhaps if we had succeeded and died in action, then
perhaps— [*A pause.*] We shall die because we were
given an idiotic assignment and because we executed
it badly. Our death serves no one. The cause didn't
need to have this village attacked. It didn't need it
because the project was impossible. A cause never
gives orders; it never says anything. It is we who
have to determine what it needs. Let's not speak of
the cause. Not here. As long as we could work for it,

it was all right. But now that we can't, we shouldn't even speak of it and above all we shouldn't use it for our personal consolation. It rejected us because we are useless to it now; it will find others to serve it. In Tours, in Lille, in Carcassonne, women are breeding the children who will take our places. We tried to justify our lives and we missed out. Now we are going to die. We'll be dead and will be unjustified corpses.

CANORIS [*indifferently*] : If you like. Nothing that happens in these four walls has any importance. Hope or despair: nothing will come of it. [*A pause.*]

HENRI : If only there were something to attempt. Anything. Or something to hide from them. Bah! [*A pause. To* CANORIS] Have you got a wife?

CANORIS : Yes. In Greece.

HENRI : Can you think of her?

CANORIS : I try. It's kind of far.

HENRI [*to* SORBIER] : How about you?

SORBIER : There are the old folks. They think I'm in England. I suppose they're just sitting down to dinner; they eat early. If I could tell myself that they're going to feel, all of a sudden, ever so lightly, a pang at the heart, a sort of presentiment— But I'm sure that they're quite calm. They'll wait for me for years, more and more unconcernedly, and I shall die in their hearts without their ever noticing. My father must be talking about his garden. He never failed to mention the garden at dinner. Soon he'll go water his cabbages. [*He sighs.*] Poor old fellow! Why should I think of them? It doesn't help.

HENRI : No. It doesn't help. [*A pause.*] Just the same, I should like it if my parents were still living. I have no one.

SORBIER : No one at all?

HENRI : No one.

LUCIE [*sharply*] : You're unfair. You have Jean. We all have Jean. He was our leader and he's thinking of us.

HENRI : He's thinking of you because he loves you.

LUCIE : He's thinking *of us all.*

HENRI [*gently*] : Did we ever talk much about our dead? We didn't have time to bury them, even in our hearts. [*A pause.*] No, I'm not missed anywhere, I haven't left any vacancy. The subways are jammed, the restaurants are packed, heads are full to bursting with petty cares. I've slipped out of the world and it has remained full. Like an egg. So it must be that I was not indispensable. [*A pause.*] I should have liked to be indispensable. To something or to someone. [*A pause.*] You know, Lucie, I was in love with you. I can tell you that now since it no longer matters.

LUCIE : No. It doesn't matter any more.

HENRI : So there it is. [*He laughs.*] It was really no use at all for me to have been born.

[*The door opens. Several troopers enter.*]

SORBIER : Hello. [*To* HENRI] They pulled this three times on us while you were sleeping.

TROOPER : Are you the one called Sorbier?

[*A moment of silence.*]

SORBIER : That's me.

TROOPER : Follow me.

◇◇

[*Again a moment of silence.*]

SORBIER : After all, I'd just as soon have them start with me. [*A pause. He walks to the door.*] I wonder if I shall get to know myself. [*As he is going out*] It's the time when my father sprinkles his cabbages.

[*He goes out with the troopers. A long silence.*]

HENRI [*to* CANORIS] : Give me a cigarette.

CANORIS : They took mine.

HENRI : Never mind. [*The music starts up again. A java is being played.*] Well, let's dance, since they want us to. Lucie?

LUCIE : I told you no.

HENRI : As you wish. There are other dancing partners. [*He goes up to the dummy, raises his handcuffed wrists and slides them over the shoulders of the dummy down to the waist. Then he begins to dance, holding the figure tight against him. The music stops.* HENRI *pauses, sets the dummy down, and then slowly raises his arms to get free of it.*] They've started.

[*They all listen.*]

CANORIS : Did you hear anything?

HENRI : Nothing.

FRANÇOIS : What do you think they're doing to him?

CANORIS : I don't know. [*A pause.*] I hope he can take it. Otherwise he'll hurt himself more than they can.

HENRI : Of course he'll take it.

CANORIS : I mean inside. It's harder when you have no information to give them. [*A pause.*]

HENRI : He hasn't cried out. That's something, anyhow.

FRANÇOIS : Perhaps they are just asking him questions.

CANORIS : Don't be ridiculous!

[SORBIER *screams. They all start.*]

LUCIE [*in a rapid, overly natural tone*] : Jean must have just arrived at Grenoble. It would surprise me if it took him more than fifteen hours. He must feel strange. The city is quiet. There are people sitting outside the cafés, and our life on the Vercors ridge is only a dream. [SORBIER's *screams grow louder.* LUCIE's *voice rises.*] He's thinking of us, he hears the radio through the open windows, the sun is shining on the mountains, it's a beautiful summer afternoon. [*Still louder cries.*] Ah! [*She lets herself fall back on a trunk, repeating between sobs:*] A beautiful summer afternoon.

HENRI [*to* CANORIS] : I won't scream.

CANORIS : You'll be wrong not to. It makes you feel better.

HENRI : I couldn't bear the idea that you were listening to me and that she was crying up here.

[FRANÇOIS *begins to shake.*]

FRANÇOIS [*on the verge of a breakdown*] : I don't believe—I don't believe— [*Steps in the corridor.*]

CANORIS : Quiet, kid, here they come.

HENRI : Who's next?

CANORIS : You or I. They'll keep the girl and the kid for last. [*The key turns in the lock.*] I hope they take me. I don't like to hear the cries of others.

[*The door opens.* JEAN *is pushed into the room. He is not handcuffed. He blinks his eyes, after entering, to get used to the darkness. They all turn toward him. The* TROOPER *leaves, shutting the door behind him.*]

LUCIE : Jean!

◇◇

JEAN : Be quiet. Don't mention my name. Come here against the wall; they may be watching us through a chink in the door. [*He looks at her.*] There you are! Right by me! I thought I should never see you again. Who's here with you?

CANORIS : Canoris.

HENRI : Henri.

JEAN : I can't see you clearly. Pierre and Jacques are—?

HENRI : Yes.

JEAN : The boy is here too? Poor kid. [*In a low and rapid tone*] I hoped you'd be dead.

HENRI [*laughing*] : We did our best.

JEAN : I don't doubt that. [*To* LUCIE] What's the matter?

LUCIE : Oh, Jean, it's all finished now. I kept telling myself: he's in Grenoble, he's walking in the streets, he's looking at the mountains. . . . And—and—now it's all over.

JEAN : Don't carry on so. I have every chance of getting out of this.

HENRI : How did they get you?

JEAN : They haven't got me yet. I ran into one of their patrols 'way down on the Verdone road. I said I was from Cimiers; that's a little town in the valley. They brought me here; I'll be held until somebody goes and checks on my story.

LUCIE : But at Cimiers they'll find out—

JEAN : I have friends there who know what to tell them. I'll get out of this. [*A pause.*] I have to; the others don't know anything about it.

HENRI [*whistles*] : That's right, too. [*A pause.*] Well,

why don't you say it? We missed our chance for fair, didn't we?

JEAN : We'll start again elsewhere.

HENRI : *You'll* start again. [*Steps in corridor.*]

CANORIS : Get away from him. They shouldn't see you talking to him.

JEAN : What's up?

HENRI : They're bringing Sorbier back.

JEAN : Ah! They—

HENRI : Yes. They began with him.

[*The* TROOPERS *enter, supporting* SORBIER, *who collapses against a trunk. The* TROOPERS *go out.*]

SORBIER [*without seeing* JEAN] : Did they keep me long?

HENRI : Half an hour.

SORBIER : Half an hour? You were right, Canoris, time goes quickly. Did you hear me scream? [*They do not reply.*] Naturally you heard me.

FRANÇOIS : What did they do to you?

SORBIER : You'll see. You'll see soon enough. Don't be in a hurry.

FRANÇOIS : Was it—very bad?

SORBIER : I don't know about that. But here's something I can tell you: they asked me where Jean is, and if I had known I would have told them. [*He laughs.*] You see: now I really know what I am like. [*They are silent.*] What's the matter? [*He follows their glance and sees* JEAN, *glued against the wall, his arms wide apart.*] Who's that? Is it Jean?

HENRI [*sharply*] : Quiet. They think he's some guy from Cimiers.

SORBIER : A guy from Cimiers? [*He sighs.*] It's just my luck.

HENRI [*surprised*] : What did you say?

SORBIER : I said it's just my luck. Now I have something to hide from them.

HENRI [*almost joyfully*] : That's true. Now we all have something to hide from them.

SORBIER : I wish they had killed me.

CANORIS : Sorbier! I swear to you that you won't talk. You *couldn't* talk.

SORBIER : I tell you, I would have given up my own mother. [*A pause.*] It's not fair that a single minute should be enough to ruin a whole life.

CANORIS [*gently*] : It takes much more than a minute. Do you think that a single moment of weakness could destroy that hour when you decided to leave everything and come with us? And these three years of courage and patience? And the day when, despite your fatigue, you carried the kid's pack and his gun?

SORBIER : Don't talk so much. Now I know. I know what I really am.

CANORIS : Why say "really"? Why should the Sorbier they beat today be more real than the one who refused to drink yesterday in order to give his share to Lucie? We're not made to live forever at our peak. There are roads in the valleys, too.

SORBIER : That's all fine. But if I had talked a little while ago, could you still look me in the eyes?

CANORIS : You won't talk.

SORBIER : But what if I do? [CANORIS *is silent.*] There, you see. [*A pause. He laughs.*] There are guys who'll die in bed, with good consciences. Good sons, good husbands, good citizens, good fathers. . . . Ha! They're weaklings like me and they'll never know it. It's just that they're lucky. [*A pause.*] Well, shut me up! What are you waiting for? Why don't you shut me up?

HENRI : Sorbier, you're the best of us.

SORBIER : Shut up!

[*There are steps in the corridor. They are all silent. The door opens.*]

TROOPER : Where is the Greek?

CANORIS : That's me.

TROOPER : Come along.

[CANORIS *goes out with the* TROOPER.]

JEAN : It's for me that he's going to suffer.

HENRI : Just as well that it's for you. Otherwise it would be for nothing.

JEAN : When he comes back, how can I look him in the eyes? [*To* LUCIE] Tell me, do you hate me?

LUCIE : Do I look as if I hate you?

JEAN : Give me your hand. [*She extends her bound hands.*] I'm ashamed not to be in handcuffs. You're here, beside me! I told myself: at least everything is over for her. An end to fear, hunger, grief. And here you are! They'll come to fetch you and they'll bring you back, half carrying you.

LUCIE : You'll see nothing in my eyes but love!

JEAN : I'll have to hear your screams.

LUCIE : I'll try not to scream.

JEAN : But the kid will scream. I know he will.

FRANÇOIS : Shut up! Shut up! All of you! Do you want

to drive me crazy? I'm not a hero and I don't want to be martyred in your place!

LUCIE: François!

FRANÇOIS: Oh, leave me alone: I don't sleep with him. [*To* JEAN] As for me, if you want to know, I hate you. [*A pause.*]

JEAN: You are right. [*He goes toward the door.*]

HENRI: Hey, there! What are you up to?

JEAN: I'm not in the habit of sending kids to be tortured in my stead.

HENRI: Who'll warn the others?

[JEAN *stops.*]

FRANÇOIS: Let him go! If he wants to give himself up. You have no right to stop him.

HENRI [*to* JEAN, *ignoring* FRANÇOIS's *outburst*]: It'll be just fine when they all come dashing up here believing we took the village. [JEAN *retraces his steps, his head bowed. He sits down.*] Better give me a cigarette. [JEAN *gives him a cigarette.*] And give me one for the kid.

FRANÇOIS: Leave me alone. [*He goes to the rear.*]

HENRI: Light it. [JEAN *lights it for him.* HENRI *takes two puffs and then sobs nervously.*] It's all right. I love to smoke, but I never knew it could give me that much pleasure. How many do you have?

JEAN: One more.

HENRI [*to* SORBIER]: Here. [SORBIER *takes the cigarette without saying a word, takes a couple of drags, and then returns it.* HENRI *turns toward* JEAN.] I'm happy you're here. First you've given me a cigarette and then you'll be our witness. You'll go see Sorbier's parents and you'll write to Canoris's wife.

LUCIE : Tomorrow you'll go down to the city; you'll take away in your eyes the last look at my face; you'll be the only one in the world to know it. You must not forget it. I am you. If you live, I shall live.

JEAN : How could I forget it! [*He approaches her. Steps in the corridor.*]

HENRI : Stay where you are and be quiet; they are coming. It's my turn and if I don't talk fast I may not have time to finish. Listen to me! If you had not appeared we should have suffered like animals, without knowing why. But you are here, and all that is to come will now have a meaning. We're going to fight. Not just for you, but for all the comrades. We missed our chance, but maybe we can save face. [*A pause.*] I thought I was utterly useless, but now I can see that I am needed for something, after all. With a bit of luck I can maybe tell myself that I'm not going to die for nothing.

[*The door opens.* CANORIS *appears, supported by* TWO TROOPERS.]

SORBIER : He didn't scream, that one.

CURTAIN

ACT II

A schoolroom. Benches and desks. White plaster walls. On the rear wall a map of Africa and a portrait of Pétain. A blackboard. To the left, a window. At the back, a door. A radio on a shelf by the window. CLOCHET, PELLERIN, LANDRIEU *are working.*

CLOCHET : Shall we go on to the next?

LANDRIEU : Just a minute. Let's take time out for a bite.

CLOCHET : Eat if you like. I could perhaps question one of them in the meantime.

LANDRIEU : No, you would like that only too well. Aren't you hungry?

CLOCHET : No.

LANDRIEU [*to* PELLERIN] : Clochet isn't hungry! [*To* CLOCHET] You must be sick.

CLOCHET : I'm never hungry when I work. [*He goes over to the radio and turns it on.*]

PELLERIN : Don't plague us with that racket.

CLOCHET [*grumbles under his breath*] : . . . who don't like music.

PELLERIN : What did you say?

CLOCHET : I said it always surprises me to find people who don't like music.

PELLERIN : I do like music. But not that sort and not here.

CLOCHET : Really? Now me, as soon as it starts up— [*With regret*] We could have played it very softly.

PELLERIN : No!

CLOCHET : You're a couple of bastards. [*A pause.*] Shall I have one of them brought in?

LANDRIEU : For God's sake, knock it off! There are three more to go yet. We'll be here till ten o'clock tonight. I get upset when I have to work on an empty stomach.

CLOCHET : In the first place, there are only two left, since we're saving the kid for tomorrow. And then, with a little organization, we could finish them off in two hours. [*A pause.*] They're broadcasting *Tosca* on Radio-Toulouse tonight.

LANDRIEU : To hell with *Tosca*. Go downstairs and see what they've dug up for us to eat.

CLOCHET : I know: chicken.

LANDRIEU : Again! I'm sick of it. Go see if you can find me a can of bully beef.

CLOCHET [*to* PELLERIN] : How about you?

PELLERIN : Beef for me too.

LANDRIEU : And get someone to wash that up.

CLOCHET : What?

LANDRIEU : Over there. Where the Greek was bleeding. It's a mess.

CLOCHET : We shouldn't clean up the blood. It might have an effect.

LANDRIEU : I can't eat with that crap on the floor. [*A pause.*] Well, what are you waiting for?

CLOCHET : I don't think we should clean it up.

LANDRIEU : Who's in charge here?

[CLOCHET *shrugs his shoulders and goes out.*]

PELLERIN : Don't ride him so hard.

LANDRIEU : I should worry about him!

PELLERIN : What I'm trying to tell you—he has a cousin close to Darnand. He sends him reports. I think he was the one who put a finger on Daubin.

LANDRIEU : The dirty bastard! If he wants to take a crack at me, he'd better hurry up about it, because I have an idea that Darnand will get his before I do.

PELLERIN : Could be. [*He sighs and goes mechanically to the radio.*]

LANDRIEU : Ah, no! Not you.

PELLERIN : Let's just hear the news.

LANDRIEU [*chuckling*] : I've got a pretty good idea what the news is.

[PELLERIN *twirls the dials of the radio.*]

ANNOUNCER'S VOICE : On the fourth musical note it will be exactly eight o'clock. [*Tone signals. They set their watches.*] Ladies and gentlemen, in a few seconds you will hear our Sunday concert.

LANDRIEU [*sighing*] : It is Sunday, that's a fact. [*The first bars of a piece of music.*] Clip him off.

PELLERIN : Sundays I used to take my jaloppy, pick up some chick in Montmartre, and take a spin to Touquet.

LANDRIEU : When was this?

PELLERIN : Oh, before the war.

SPEAKER : I found nails in the vicar's garden. We repeat: I found . . .

LANDRIEU : Shut the hell up, you filthy bastards! [*He picks up a can of food and throws it in the direction of the radio.*]

PELLERIN: Are you nuts? You'll smash the radio.

LANDRIEU: I don't give a damn. I can't stand that crap. [PELLERIN *turns the dial.*]

SPEAKER: The German troops are holding firmly at Cherbourg and at Caen. In the Saint-Lô sector they have not been able to check a slight advance by the enemy.

LANDRIEU: We get it. Turn it off. [*A pause.*] What will you do? Where will you go?

PELLERIN: What do you think? We're cooked.

LANDRIEU: Yes. The dirty bastards!

PELLERIN: Who do you mean?

LANDRIEU: All of 'em. The Germans, too. They're all the same. [*A pause.*] If it could be done all over again—

PELLERIN: Oh, I don't regret anything. I had a good time, at least up till these last few weeks.

[CLOCHET *enters, bringing the canned meat.*]

LANDRIEU: Hey, Clochet, the British have landed at Nice.

CLOCHET: At Nice?

LANDRIEU: And they met no resistance. They are marching on Puget-Théniers.

[CLOCHET *sinks down on one of the benches.*]

CLOCHET: Holy Mother! [LANDRIEU *and* PELLERIN *begin to laugh.*] You're kidding? But you shouldn't make jokes like that.

LANDRIEU: O.K. You can put that in your report tonight. [A TROOPER *enters.*] Clean up that mess over there. [*To* PELLERIN] Are you going to eat with me?

[PELLERIN *goes up to him, takes the can of beef, looks at it, then puts it down.*]

PELLERIN [*he yawns*] : I always feel kind of funny before we start. [*He yawns.*] I guess I'm just not nasty enough; I can't get into the spirit of it unless they're stubborn. What's he like, the guy we're going to question?

CLOCHET : A big fellow, about thirty, solidly built. It'll be fun.

LANDRIEU : Let's hope he doesn't act like the Greek.

PELLERIN : Hell! The Greek was a big, dumb ape.

LANDRIEU : Just the same. It fouls you up when they don't talk. [*He yawns.*] You're making me yawn. [*A pause.* LANDRIEU *looks at the bottom of his can of beef, not speaking. Then he turns suddenly to the* TROOPER.] All right, go fetch him.

[*The* TROOPER *goes out. Silence.* CLOCHET *whistles softly.* PELLERIN *goes to the window and opens it wide.*]

CLOCHET : Don't open the window. It's getting chilly.

PELLERIN : What window? Oh, yes. [*He laughs.*] I opened it without thinking. [*He goes to close it.*]

LANDRIEU : Leave it open. It's stifling in here, I need air.

CLOCHET : As you wish.

[*Enter* HENRI *and three* TROOPERS.]

LANDRIEU : Put him there. Take off his handcuffs. Tie his hands to the arms of the chair. [*The* TROOPERS *fasten his hands.*] Your name?

HENRI : Henri.

LANDRIEU : Henri what?

HENRI : Henri.

[LANDRIEU *gives a sign and the* TROOPERS *strike* HENRI.]

LANDRIEU: Now. What's your name.

HENRI: I'm Henri, just Henri.

[*They strike him.*]

LANDRIEU: Stop, you'll make him too groggy to talk. How old are you?

HENRI: Twenty-nine.

LANDRIEU: Profession?

HENRI: Before the war I was a medical student.

PELLERIN: You're an educated bastard. [*To the* TROOPERS] Let him have it.

LANDRIEU: Let's not waste time.

PELLERIN: A medical student, eh! Well, let him have it!

LANDRIEU: Pellerin! [*To* HENRI] Where's your chief?

HENRI: I don't know.

LANDRIEU: Of course. No, don't hit him. Do you smoke? Give him this cigarette. Wait, [*He puts it in his own mouth, lights it, and hands it to a* TROOPER, *who puts it in* HENRI's *mouth.*] Go on, smoke. What can you hope for? You don't impress us. Come, Henri, don't show off; nobody is watching you. Save your time and ours; you don't have very many hours to live.

HENRI: Nor do you.

LANDRIEU: Well, we can still count it in months. Enough time to bury you. Smoke up. And think. Since you're educated, be realistic. If you don't talk, it will be the girl friend or the kid.

HENRI: That's their business.

LANDRIEU: Where is your chief?

HENRI : Try to make me tell you.

LANDRIEU : You prefer that? Take away his cigarette. Clochet, fix him up.

CLOCHET : Put sticks in the ropes. [*The* TROOPERS *slip two sticks in the ropes that bind* HENRI'S *wrists.*] Good. They'll turn until you talk.

HENRI : I won't talk.

CLOCHET : Not right away: you'll scream first.

HENRI : Try to make me.

CLOCHET : You're not humble. One must be humble. If you fall from too high up you break your neck. Turn. Slowly. Well? Nothing? No. Turn, turn. Wait: he is beginning to feel pain. Well? No? Of course: pain doesn't exist for a man of your education. The pity is that we can see it in your face. [*Softly*] You're sweating. I'm sorry for you. [*He wipes* HENRI'S *face with a handkerchief.*] Turn. Will he yell? Won't he yell? You're wriggling. You can keep from crying, but you can't keep your head from wriggling. How bad you must feel! [*He passes his fingers over* HENRI'S *cheeks.*] How you grit your teeth! Are you scared? "If I could hold out a minute longer, only one little minute. . . ." But after this minute will come another, and then another still, until you find the pain too great and then you'll think it's better to despise yourself. We won't let you off. [*He takes his head in his hands.*] These eyes no longer see me now. What is it they see? [*Softly*] You are handsome. Turn. [*A pause. With triumph*] You're going to scream, Henri, you're going to scream. I can see the cry swelling your neck; it's rising to your lips. Just a

little more pressure. Turn. [HENRI *screams.*] Ha!
[*A pause.*] How ashamed you must be! Turn. Don't
stop. [HENRI *screams out again.*] You see; it is only
the first scream that comes hard. Now gently, very
naturally, you'll talk.

HENRI : You'll get nothing from me but screams.

CLOCHET : No, Henri, no. You no longer have the right
to be proud. "Try to make me scream!" You saw;
it didn't take long. Where is your chief? Be humble,
Henri, really humble. Tell us where he is. Very well,
what are you waiting for? Scream or speak. Turn.
Turn, damn it; break his wrists. Stop: he's passed out.
[*He goes to get a bottle of whisky and a glass. Almost
tenderly he makes* HENRI *drink.*] Drink, poor martyr.
Do you feel better? Good, we can start again. Go
get the tools.

LANDRIEU : No!

CLOCHET : How's that?

[LANDRIEU *rubs his hand over his brow.*]

LANDRIEU : Take him out. You can work on him down
there.

CLOCHET : We'll be cramped for room.

LANDRIEU : I'm in command here, Clochet. This is the
second time I've had to remind you.

CLOCHET : But—

LANDRIEU [*shouting*] : Do you want a punch in the
nose?

CLOCHET : All right, all right, take him along.

[*The* TROOPERS *unfasten* HENRI *and carry him out.*
CLOCHET *follows.*]

PELLERIN : Are you coming?

◇◇

LANDRIEU : No. Clochet disgusts me.

PELLERIN : He talks too much. [*A pause.*] A medical student, if you please! The bastard. I had to leave school at thirteen to earn a living. I wasn't lucky enough to have rich parents to pay for me to study.

LANDRIEU : I hope he talks.

PELLERIN : Good Christ, yes; he'll talk!

LANDRIEU : That fouls it up, a guy who won't talk.

[HENRI *screams.* LANDRIEU *goes to the door and shuts it. More cries, which can be heard clearly through the door.* LANDRIEU *goes to the radio and turns it on.*]

PELLERIN [*astounded*] : You, too, Landrieu?

LANDRIEU : It's those screams. You have to have nerves like iron.

PELLERIN : Let him scream. He's a bastard, a dirty intellectual. [*Strident music.*] Not so loud. I can't hear.

LANDRIEU : Go join them. [PELLERIN *hesitates, then goes out.*] He'll have to talk. He's a coward, he must be a coward. [*Music and screams. The screams stop. A pause.* PELLERIN *come in again, pale.*]

PELLERIN : Stop the music. [LANDRIEU *turns off the radio.*]

LANDRIEU : Well?

PELLERIN : They'll kill him before he talks.

LANDRIEU [*goes to the door*] : Stop it. Bring him in here.

[*The* TROOPERS *bring in* HENRI. CLOCHET *is at his side.*]

PELLERIN [*goes up to* HENRI] : We're not through with you yet. We can begin where we left off, never fear.

Lower your eyes. I tell you, lower your eyes. [*He strikes him.*] You pig!

CLOCHET [*approaching* HENRI] : Hold out your hands, I'm going to put the cuffs on. [*He adjusts the handcuffs very gently.*] It hurts, doesn't it? Hurts a lot, eh? Poor little boy. [*He strokes his hair.*] Come on, now, don't be so proud. You screamed, you screamed, anyway. Tomorrow you'll talk.

[*At a gesture from* LANDRIEU, *the* TROOPERS *lead* HENRI *out.*]

PELLERIN : The bastard!

LANDRIEU : That fouls it up.

PELLERIN : What?

LANDRIEU : It fouls things up when a guy won't talk.

CLOCHET : Well, he screamed, anyhow. I got him to scream. [*He shrugs his shoulders.*]

PELLERIN : Bring the girl.

LANDRIEU : The girl—if she doesn't talk—

PELLERIN : Well—

LANDRIEU : Nothing. [*With sudden violence*] There *must* be one of them who'll talk.

CLOCHET : We should have the blond fellow sent down. He's ripe.

LANDRIEU : The blond one?

CLOCHET : Sorbier. He's a coward.

LANDRIEU : A coward? Go get him.

[CLOCHET *goes out.*]

PELLERIN : They're all cowards. Only some of them are stubborn.

LANDRIEU : Pellerin! What would you do if they tore out your nails?

◇◇

PELLERIN : The British don't tears out nails.

LANDRIEU : What about the Maquis?

PELLERIN : They won't tear our nails out.

LANDRIEU : Why not?

PELLERIN : Things like that can't happen to us.

[CLOCHET *enters, followed by* SORBIER, *accompanied by* TROOPERS.]

CLOCHET : Let me question him. Remove his handcuffs. Tie his arms to the chair. Good. [*He goes up to* SORBIER.] Ah, yes, so here you are. Here you are once more in this chair. And here we are too. Do you know why we had you brought down?

SORBIER : No.

CLOCHET : Because you're a coward and you're going to squeal. You are a coward, aren't you?

SORBIER : Yes.

CLOCHET : There you are, you see. I read it in your eyes. Show me those big staring eyes.

SORBIER : Your eyes will look like that when they hang you.

CLOCHET : Don't show off now; it doesn't suit you very well.

SORBIER : The same eyes; we're brothers. I attract you, isn't that so? It's not me you are torturing. It's yourself.

CLOCHET [*abruptly*] : You're a Jew, aren't you?

SORBIER [*surprised*] : Me? No.

CLOCHET : And I say that you are a Jew. [*At a sign from* CLOCHET, *the* TROOPERS *strike* SORBIER.] Aren't you a Jew?

SORBIER : Yes. I am a Jew.

CLOCHET : Good. Now listen carefully. We'll start with the nails. That will give you time to make up your mind. We're not in a hurry, we have all night! Are you going to talk?

SORBIER : What dirt!

CLOCHET : What did you say?

SORBIER : I said: what dirt. You and I are both just dirt.

CLOCHET [*to the* TROOPERS] : Take the pincers and begin.

SORBIER : Let me go! Let me go! I'll talk. I'll tell you all you want to know.

CLOCHET [*to the* TROOPERS] : Pull the nail a bit anyhow, so he'll know we mean business. [SORBIER *groans.*] O.K., where's your leader?

SORBIER : Untie me, I can't sit in this chair. Not any more! Not any more! [*A sign from* LANDRIEU. *The* TROOPERS *unfasten him. He gets up and staggers to the table.*] Give me a cigarette.

LANDRIEU : Later.

SORBIER : What do you want to know? Where our leader is? I know. None of the others do, but I really know. He confided in me. He is— [*Pointing suddenly behind them*] there! [*All turn around. He leaps to the window and jumps up on the ledge.*] I won! Come near and I jump. I won! I won!

CLOCHET : Don't be a fool. If you talk we'll let you off.

SORBIER : Don't feed me that line! [*Shouting*] Hey, up there! Henri, Canoris, I didn't talk! [*The* TROOPERS *make a grab for him. He leaps out of the window.*] Good night!

PELLERIN : The bastard! The dirty coward! [*They lean out of the window.*]

LANDRIEU [*to the* TROOPERS] : Go on down. If he's alive, bring him back up. We'll put the heat on him until he cracks. [*The* TROOPERS *go out. A pause.*]

CLOCHET : I told you to close the window.

[LANDRIEU *goes up to him and punches him in the face.*]

LANDRIEU : You can put that in your report.

[*A pause.* CLOCHET *takes out his handkerchief and wipes his mouth. The* TROOPERS *come back in.*]

TROOPER : Dead as a mackerel.

LANDRIEU : The dirty whore! [*To the* TROOPERS] Go get me the girl. [*The* TROOPERS *go out.*] They'll talk, by Christ! They'll talk!

CURTAIN

ACT III

The attic. FRANÇOIS, CANORIS, HENRI *are seated on the floor in a semicircle. They form a closely knit group. They talk in half-tones.* JEAN *walks around them, evidently miserable. From time to time he seems about to enter the conversation, but then catches himself and continues his walking.*

CANORIS : When they were tying me up, I watched them. A guy came up and hit me. I looked at him and thought: I've seen that face somewhere. After that they went to work on me and I tried to remember him.

HENRI : Which one of them was it?

CANORIS : The big fellow who talks so much. I've seen him in Grenoble. You know Chasières, the baker on the rue Longue? He sells cream-puffs in his back room. Every Sunday morning this guy would come out of the place carrying a package of cakes bound with a pink string. I remembered him because of his ugly mug. I thought he was working for the police.

HENRI : You might have told me that before.

CANORIS : That he was with the police?

HENRI : That Chasières sold cream-puffs. Did he feed you a line, too?

CANORIS : I should say so. He had leaned over me and was breathing in my face.

JEAN [*breaking into the conversation*] : What did he

say? [*They turn toward him with evident surprise.*]

CANORIS : Nothing. A lot of crap.

JEAN : I don't think I could take that.

HENRI : Why not? It's amusing.

JEAN : Oh! Oh! Yes? Naturally, I couldn't very well
appreciate that.

[*A silence.* HENRI *turns to* CANORIS.]

HENRI : What do you think they do in private life?

CANORIS : The big fat one who took notes could be a
dentist.

HENRI : Not bad. Say, it's lucky he didn't bring his drill.
[*They laugh.*]

JEAN [*violently*] : Don't laugh. [*They stop laughing
and look at him.*] I know: you can laugh, sure you
can. You have a right to laugh. And besides, I have no
more orders to give you. [*A pause.*] If you had told
me that one day I would be afraid of you— [*A
pause.*] But how can you be so gay?

HENRI : We manage.

JEAN : Naturally. You're suffering on your own score.
That's what gives a man a clear conscience. I was
married; I never told you. My wife died in child-
birth. I paced the hall of the hospital and I knew she
would die. It's the same story, exactly the same! I
wanted to help her, and I couldn't. I paced back and
forth listening for her cries. She didn't make a sound.
She had the better role. Like you.

HENRI : That's not our fault.

JEAN : Nor mine. I'd like to help you if I could.

CANORIS : But you can't.

JEAN : I know that. [*A pause.*] It's two hours since they took her out. They didn't keep you that long.

HENRI : She's a woman. With women they can really have a good time.

JEAN [*with a burst of violence*] : I'll come back. In a week, in a month, I'll be back. I'll have my men castrate them.

HENRI : You're lucky to still be able to hate them.

JEAN : Is that luck? Besides, I suppose I hate them mainly to give myself something to think about. [*He paces back and forth, and then, having hit on some idea, drags an old stove under the window.*]

CANORIS : You bother me. What are you up to now?

JEAN : I want to see him once more before dark.

HENRI : Who?

JEAN : Sorbier.

HENRI [*with indifference*] : Oh.
  [JEAN *climbs on the stove and looks out the window.*]

JEAN : He's still there. They'll let him rot there. Do you want to get up? I'll help you.

CANORIS : What for?

JEAN : Yes, what for? You leave the dead to me.

FRANÇOIS : I want to look.

HENRI : I advise you not to.

FRANÇOIS [*to* JEAN] : Help me up. [JEAN *helps* FRAN-ÇOIS *up. He looks out the window.*] His—his skull is all smashed. [*He climbs down and squats trembling in a corner.*]

HENRI [*to* JEAN] : That was certainly smart.

JEAN : So what? I should think, you being so tough, that you could bear the sight of a corpse.

HENRI : I could, maybe, but not the kid. [*To* FRANÇOIS] The funeral orations are Jean's department. You have no responsibility for that corpse. It is all over for him; for him it's silence. But you still have a way to go yet. Think of yourself.

FRANÇOIS : This head will be smashed open, and these eyes—

HENRI : That won't mean anything to you: you won't be there to see yourself. [*A pause.* JEAN *paces back and forth and then comes to a halt before* HENRI *and* CANORIS.]

JEAN : Do they have to tear out my nails for me to be your friend again?

CANORIS : You're still our friend.

JEAN : You know better. [*A pause.*] How do you know that I wouldn't have held out? [*To* HENRI] Maybe I wouldn't have screamed.

HENRI : Well?

JEAN : Forgive me. I should only keep quiet.

HENRI : Jean! Come sit with us. [JEAN *hesitates and then sits down.*] You would be just like us if you were in our place. But we haven't the same worries. [JEAN *gets up suddenly.*] What's the matter?

JEAN : Until they bring her back, I can't sit still.

HENRI : You see what I mean; you're fidgety, you're trembling; you're too much alive.

JEAN : I went six months without telling her I loved her. The night I finally took her in my arms, I turned off the light. Now she is there with them, naked, and they're sliding their hands over her body.

HENRI : What does that matter? The important thing is to win.

JEAN : To win what?

HENRI : Just to win. There are two teams: one wants to make the other talk. [*He laughs.*] It's ridiculous, but it's all we have left. If we talk, we lose everything. They have run up a few points because I screamed, but on the whole we're not in such a bad position.

JEAN : I don't give a damn about winning or losing! That's nothing. But her shame is real; her suffering is real.

HENRI : So what? I felt shame, too, when they made me scream. But that doesn't last. If she's silent, their hands won't mark her. They're a sorry lot, those guys, you know.

JEAN : They're men and she's in their arms.

HENRI : Never mind. If you want to know, I love her myself.

JEAN : You?

HENRI : Why not? And I didn't feel much like laughing the night you both went upstairs together. I often wondered about the lights; I wondered whether you turned them off.

JEAN : You love her? And yet you can sit here calmly?

HENRI : Her pain brings her nearer to us. The pleasure you gave her separated us more. Today I am closer to her than you are.

JEAN : That's not true! It's not true! She's thinking of

me even while they torture her. She is thinking only
of me. It's so as not to surrender me that she's ready
to endure torture and shame.

HENRI : No, it's in order to win.

JEAN : You're lying! [*A pause.*] She said: "When I return there'll be only love in my eyes."

[*Steps in the corridor.*]

HENRI : She's coming back. You can look in her eyes
and find out.

[*The door opens.* HENRI *gets to his feet.* LUCIE *enters.*
JEAN *and* HENRI *look at her in silence. She passes right
by them without turning her head and sits down at
the front of the stage. A pause.*]

LUCIE : François! [FRANÇOIS *goes to her and sits against
her knees.*] Don't touch me. Give me Sorbier's coat.
[FRANÇOIS *picks up the coat.*] Throw it across my
shoulders. [*She wraps it tightly around her.*]

FRANÇOIS : Are you cold?

LUCIE : No. [*A pause.*] What's going on? Are they
looking at me? Why don't they go on talking?

JEAN [*coming up behind her*] : Lucie!

CANORIS : Leave her alone.

JEAN : Lucie!

LUCIE [*gently*] : What is it?

JEAN : You promised me there would be nothing but
love in your eyes.

LUCIE : Love? [*She shrugs her shoulders sadly.*]

CANORIS [*who has got to his feet*] : Let her be; you can
talk to her after a while.

JEAN [*violently*] : Get the hell out of this. She's mine.
You've cast me aside, both of you, and I can't say

anything; but you can't take her from me. [*To* LUCIE] Speak to me. You're not like them, are you? It's not possible you've become like them. Why don't you answer me? Are you angry with me?

LUCIE : I'm not angry with you.

JEAN : My sweet Lucie.

LUCIE : I shall never be sweet again, Jean.

JEAN : You don't love me any more.

LUCIE : I don't know. [*He takes a step toward her.*] Please, don't touch me. [*With an effort*] I think I must still love you. But I no longer feel my love. [*Wearily*] I no longer feel anything.

CANORIS [*to* JEAN] : Come away. [*He drags him away and forces him to sit down next to him.*]

LUCIE [*as if to herself*] : It's all so unimportant. [*To* FRANÇOIS] What are they doing?

FRANÇOIS : They're sitting with their backs to us.

LUCIE : Good. [*A pause.*] Tell them I didn't talk.

CANORIS : We know that, Lucie.

LUCIE : Good. [*A long pause. Then steps in the corridor.* FRANÇOIS *springs to his feet with a cry of alarm.*] What's wrong? Oh, yes, it's your turn. Do a good job: they need to be put to shame. [*The steps come closer, then move away.*]

FRANÇOIS [*throwing himself at* LUCIE's *knees*] : I can't stand it any more! I can't stand it any more!

LUCIE : Look at me! [*She raises his head.*] How frightened you were! You're not going to tell them anything? Answer me!

FRANÇOIS : I don't know now. I had a little courage left, but I shouldn't have seen you like this. Here you are, your hair disordered, your blouse torn, and I know that they took you in their arms.

LUCIE [*with violence*] : They didn't touch me. Nobody touched me. I was like stone and I didn't feel their hands. I looked them in the face and I thought: nothing is happening. [*Passionately*] And nothing did happen. In the end they were afraid of me. [*A pause.*] François, if you talk, they will really have violated me. They'll say: "We've finally had them." The memory will make them smile. They'll say: "We sure had fun with that babe." We must shame them. If I didn't hope to see them again I'd hang myself from the bars of that window this minute. You won't talk, will you? [FRANÇOIS *shrugs his shoulders without replying. A pause.*]

HENRI [*in a low voice*] : Well, Jean, who was right? She wants to win; that's all.

JEAN : Be quiet! Why do you want to take her from me? You're sitting on top of the world; you'll die happy and proud. But I have only her and I'm going to live!

HENRI : I don't want anything, and anyhow I wasn't the one who took her from you.

JEAN : Go on! Go on! You have every right to, you even have the right to torture me; you paid in advance. [*He gets to his feet.*] How sure you are of yourselves. Is suffering with your body enough to give you a clear conscience? [HENRI *does not answer.*] Can't you understand that I am more unhappy than any of you?

FRANÇOIS [*who has suddenly got to his feet*] : Ha! Ha! Ha!

JEAN [*shouting*] : The most unhappy! The most unhappy!

FRANÇOIS [*springing toward* JEAN] : Look at him! Just look at him! The most unhappy of us all. He has eaten and slept. His hands are free. He will see the sun again. He's going to live. But he's the most unhappy. What do you want? Someone to pity you too, you bastard?

JEAN [*crossing his arms*] : Good!

FRANÇOIS : I jump out of my skin at every sound. The spit sticks in my throat, I'm dying. But he is the most unhappy of all. Sure! And I shall die in rapture! [*Vehemently*] Well, I'll give your happiness back to you, if that's what you want!

LUCIE [*springing to her feet*] : François!

FRANÇOIS : I'll denounce you! I'll denounce you! I'll let you share our joys!

JEAN [*in a low and rapid tone*] : Go ahead. You couldn't know how much I want you to.

LUCIE [*taking* FRANÇOIS *by the back of the neck and turning his head toward her*] : Look me in the face. Would you dare talk?

FRANÇOIS : Dare! Your big words again. I'll just denounce him, that's all. It'll be so simple, they'll come for me and my mouth will open all by itself. The name will pop out just like that, and I'll agree with my mouth. What's there to dare? When I see you pale and on edge, acting like a maniac, your scorn doesn't frighten me any more. [*A pause.*] I'll save you, Lucie. They'll let us live.

LUCIE : I don't want that kind of life.

FRANÇOIS : Well, I do. I want any kind of life. Shame passes when you live long enough.

CANORIS : They'll show you no mercy, François. Even if you talk.

FRANÇOIS [*pointing at* JEAN] : At least I'll see him suffer.

HENRI [*rises and goes over to* LUCIE] : Do you think he'll talk?

LUCIE [*turns toward* FRANÇOIS *and stares at him*] : Yes.

HENRI : Are you sure? [*They look at each other.*]

LUCIE [*after a long hesitation*] : Yes.

[HENRI *goes toward* FRANÇOIS. CANORIS *gets up and stands beside* HENRI. *Both stare at* FRANÇOIS.]

HENRI : It is not for me to judge you, François. You're just a kid, and this whole business is too tough for you. At your age I think I would have talked, too.

CANORIS : It's all our fault. We shouldn't have taken you with us; there are some risks that only men should take. Please forgive us.

FRANÇOIS [*recoiling*] : What do you mean? What are you going to do to me?

HENRI : You must not talk, François. They'll kill you all the same, you know. And you'll die in despair.

FRANÇOIS [*frightened*] : All right then, I won't talk. I tell you I won't talk. Let me go.

HENRI : We can't trust you any longer. They know that you're our weak point. They'll work on you without let-up until you come clean. It's up to us to keep you from talking.

JEAN : Do you suppose I'll stand by and let you do this? Don't worry, kid. My hands are free, and I am with you.

LUCIE [*barring the way*] : Why don't you keep out of this?

JEAN : He's your brother.

LUCIE : So? He'll die tomorrow anyway.

JEAN : Is this really you? You frighten me.

LUCIE : He must not talk. The means doesn't count.

FRANÇOIS : You're not going to— [*They don't answer him.*] But I told you I won't talk. [*They don't reply.*] Lucie, help, keep them from hurting me; I won't talk; I swear to you I won't talk.

JEAN [*placing himself beside* FRANÇOIS] : Don't lay a hand on him.

HENRI : Jean, when are our comrades due to arrive in the village?

JEAN : Tuesday.

HENRI : How many are they?

JEAN : Sixty.

HENRI : Sixty men who trust you and who on Tuesday will die like rats. It's them or him. Choose.

JEAN : You have no right to ask me to choose.

HENRI : Aren't you their leader? Well!

[JEAN *hesitates a moment and then slowly steps aside.* HENRI *approaches* FRANÇOIS.]

FRANÇOIS [*watches him and then begins to scream*] : Lucie! Help! I don't want to die here, not in this blackness. Henri, I'm fifteen, let me live. Don't kill

me in the dark. [HENRI *takes him by the throat.*]
Lucie! [LUCIE *turns her head away.*] I hate you all.

LUCIE : My little one, my poor darling, my only love,
forgive us. [*She turns away. A pause.*] Make it quick.

HENRI : I can't. They've half broken my wrists. [*A
pause.*]

LUCIE : Is it done?

HENRI : He's dead.

[LUCIE *turns and takes* FRANÇOIS's *body in her arms.
His head rests on her knees. A very long silence, then*
JEAN *begins to talk in a low voice. All the conversa-
tion that follows is in a low voice.*]

JEAN : What has happened to you all? Why didn't you
die with the others? You horrify me.

HENRI : Do you think I love myself?

JEAN : All right. In twenty-four hours you'll be rid of
yourself. But every day from now on I'll see that kid
begging for mercy and I'll see your face as those
hands tightened about his throat. [*He goes to* FRAN-
ÇOIS *and looks at him.*] Fifteen years old! And he died
mad with fear. [*He turns toward* HENRI.] He loved
you. He slept with his head on your shoulder. He
used to say: "I sleep better when you're there." [*A
pause.*] You bastard!

HENRI [*to* CANORIS *and* LUCIE] : Well, why don't you
speak up? Don't leave me alone. Lucie! Canoris! You
killed him with my hands. [*No answer. He turns
toward* JEAN.] And you, who have set yourself up
as my judge, what did you do to save him?

JEAN [*with violence*] : What could I do? What would
you have let me do?

HENRI: Your hands were free, you should have hit me. [*Passionately*] If you had hit me—if you had beaten me till I fell—

JEAN: My hands were free? You had me tied hand and foot. If I make a move, if I say a word, then: "What about the comrades?" You excluded me, you've decided my life and my death, coldly. Don't come telling me now that I'm your accomplice; that would be too easy. I'm your witness, no more. And I am a witness that you are murderers. [*A pause.*] You killed him out of pride.

HENRI: You lie!

JEAN: Out of pride! They made you scream, didn't they? And you were ashamed. You want to dazzle them, to redeem yourself; you want to save for yourself a heroic death. Isn't that true? You want to win, you told us. You told us that you wanted to win.

HENRI: That's not true! That's not true! Lucie, tell him that it's not true! [LUCIE *does not answer. He takes a step toward her.*] Answer me: do you think I killed him out of pride?

LUCIE: I don't know. [*A pause. Then laboriously*] We had to keep him from talking.

HENRI: Do you hate me? He was your brother; you alone have the right to condemn me.

LUCIE: I don't hate you. [*He leans over the body she holds in her arms. Vehemently*] Don't touch him. [HENRI *slowly turns and goes back toward* CANORIS.]

HENRI: Canoris! You didn't scream, yet you wanted him to die, too. Did we kill him out of pride?

CANORIS : I have no pride.

HENRI : But I do! It's true that I do have pride. Did I kill him out of pride?

CANORIS : You ought to know.

HENRI : I— No, I don't know any more. Everything happened too fast and now he's dead. [*Abruptly*] Don't leave me! You have no right to leave me. When my hands were around his throat, it seemed to me that they were our hands and that we were all pressing together, otherwise I should never have been capable of—

CANORIS : He had to die. If he had stood nearer me, I would have done it. As for what's going on in your head—

HENRI : Yes?

CANORIS : That doesn't count. Nothing counts within these four walls. He had to die; that's all there is to it.

HENRI : All right. [*He comes up to the body. To* LUCIE] Don't be afraid, I won't touch him. [*He leans over the body and stares at it for some time, then straightens up.*] Jean, when we threw the first grenade, how many hostages did they shoot? [JEAN *doesn't answer.*] Twelve. There was a kid in the lot, a kid named Destaches. You must remember; we saw the posters in the rue des Minimes. Charbonnel wanted to give himself up and you wouldn't let him.

JEAN : Well?

HENRI : Did you ask yourself why you wouldn't let him?

JEAN : That was different.

HENRI : Perhaps. All the better for you if your motives were clearer: you have nothing on your conscience. But Destaches is dead just the same. I'll never again have a clear conscience, never until they prop me against a wall with a handkerchief over my eyes. But why should I want a clear conscience? The kid had to die.

JEAN : I wouldn't want to be in your shoes.

HENRI [*gently*] : You're out of this, Jean; you can neither judge nor understand.

[*A long silence. Then* LUCIE *speaks. She caresses* FRANÇOIS's *hair, but doesn't look at him. For the first time since the beginning of the scene she raises her voice to its normal pitch.*]

LUCIE : You're dead and my eyes are dry. Forgive me; I guess I have no more tears and death no longer matters to me. Outside there are three hundred lying dead in the grass, and tomorrow I too will be cold and naked, without even a hand to fondle my hair. There's nothing to regret, you know: life itself is not so important any more. Good-by. You went as far as you could. If you stopped halfway, it is because you didn't have the strength to go farther. No one has the right to blame you.

JEAN : No one. [*A long silence. He sits down beside* LUCIE.] Lucie. [*She shrinks back.*] Don't push me away, I want to help you.

LUCIE [*astonished*] : Help me how? I don't need help.

JEAN : Yes. I think you do; I'm afraid that you'll break down.

LUCIE : I can last until tomorrow night.

JEAN : You're too tense, you'll snap. Your courage will leave you all of a sudden.

LUCIE : Why bother about me? [*She looks at him.*] You're suffering. All right, I'll reassure you and then you can go. Everything has become quite simple now that the kid is dead; I have only myself to think of. And I don't need courage to die, you know; I don't think I could have lived very long without him anyhow. Now go away. I'll say good-by to you later when they come for me.

JEAN : Let me sit near you. I'll be quiet, if you like, but I'll be there and you won't feel alone.

LUCIE : Not alone? With you? Oh, Jean, didn't you understand? We have nothing in common any more.

JEAN : Have you forgotten that I love you?

LUCIE : It was someone else you loved.

JEAN : It's you.

LUCIE : I'm somebody else. I don't even recognize myself. Something must have got blocked up in my head.

JEAN : Perhaps. Perhaps you are another person. In that case it's this other person that I love now, and tomorrow I shall love the dead person you will be. It's you I love, Lucie, *you*, happy or unhappy, alive or dead. It's you.

LUCIE : All right. You love me. So?

JEAN : You loved me too.

LUCIE : Yes. And I loved my brother, whom I let them kill. Our love is so far away, why should you speak to me of it? It really wasn't important.

JEAN : That's a lie! You know very well that you're

lying. It was our whole life, no more and no less than our whole life. Everything that happened we went through together.

LUCIE : Our whole life, yes. Our future. I lived in expectation, I loved you in hope. I waited only for the end of the war, for the day we could be married before everyone. I waited for you each night. Now I have no future; I wait only for my death and I shall die alone. [*A pause.*] Leave me alone. We have nothing to say to each other; I'm not suffering and I don't need consolation.

JEAN : Do you suppose I am trying to console you? I see your dry eyes and I know that your heart is an inferno; not a trace of suffering, not even the moisture of a tear, everything is white-hot. How you must suffer from not suffering! Oh, I've thought a hundred times of torture, I've felt it all in advance, but I never imagined it could produce this horrible suffering of pride. Lucie, I'd like to give you a little self-pity. If you could only relax that rigid head, if you could rest it on my shoulder. But answer me! Look at me!

LUCIE : Don't touch me.

JEAN : It's no use, Lucie, we're riveted together. All they've done to you they've done to both of us. This pain that escapes you is mine too; it waits for you. If you come into my arms it will become *our* pain. Trust me, darling, and we'll be able to say "we" again; we'll be a couple, we'll bear everything together, even your death. If you could only summon up one tear—

◇◇◇

LUCIE [*violently*] : A tear? I only wish they'd come for me again and beat me so that I could once again refuse to talk and mock them and frighten them. Everything here is so pointless: this waiting, your love, the weight of this head on my knees. I wish that grief could consume me, I'd like to burn, to say nothing and see their eyes ever watching.

JEAN [*overwhelmed*] : You're nothing but a desert of pride.

LUCIE : Am I to blame for that? It was my pride that they struck. I hate them, but they hold me. And I hold them too. I feel nearer to them than to you. [*She laughs.*] "We!" You want me to say "we." Have your wrists been smashed like Henri's? Are your legs wounded like Canoris's? Come now, this is just a comedy: you haven't felt a thing; you imagine it all.

JEAN : Smashed wrists. Ah! If that's all you want, to let me be one of you, why then it's soon done. [*He looks around, spies a heavy andiron, and seizes it.* LUCIE *bursts into laughter.*]

LUCIE : What are you up to?

JEAN [*flattens his left hand on the floor and strikes it with the andiron he holds in his right*] : I've had enough of hearing you vaunt your griefs as if they were virtues. I'm tired of looking at you with your pitiable eyes. What they've done to you I can do to myself; anybody can do it.

LUCIE [*laughing*] : It won't work, it's no use. You can break your bones, you can tear out your eyes; but it is you and you alone who are deciding what you're to suffer. Each of our hurts is a violation because it was other men who inflicted them on us. You can't catch up with us. [*A pause.* JEAN *throws away the andiron and looks at it. He gets to his feet.*]

JEAN : You're right; I can't become one of you. You're together and I'm alone. I won't stir again, I'll never speak to you again, I'll just hide in a dark corner and you'll forget that I exist. I suppose that's my part in this story and I must accept it as you accept yours. [*A pause.*] A moment ago an idea came to me: Pierre was killed near the Servaz cave where we kept arms. If they release me, I'll go hunt up his body, put some papers in his coat, and drag the body into the cave. Count four hours after I leave, and when they question you again, reveal that as the hide-away. They'll find Pierre and believe it's me. Then they'll have no further reason for torturing you and they'll finish with you quickly. That's all. Good-by. [*He goes to the rear. A long silence. Then steps in the corridor. A* TROOPER *enters with a lantern; he swings his lantern all over the room.*]

TROOPER [*catching sight of* FRANÇOIS] : What's wrong with him?

LUCIE : He's sleeping.

TROOPER [*to* JEAN] : You come along. Something new for you.

[JEAN *hesitates, looks at the others with a kind of despair, and follows the* TROOPER. *The door closes after them.*]

LUCIE : He's in the clear, don't you think?

CANORIS : I suppose so.

LUCIE : Good. That's one worry less. He'll find his kind and it will be for the best. Come here. [HENRI *and* CANORIS *come closer to her.*] Closer. Now we're amongst ourselves. Why do you hold back? [*She looks at them and grasps what they are thinking.*] Oh. [*A pause.*] He had to die; you know very well that he had to die. The ones downstairs killed him with our hands. Look, I'm his sister and I tell you that you're not guilty. Touch him; now that he's dead, he's one of us. See what a hard look he has. He has closed his lips on a secret. Touch him.

HENRI [*stroking* FRANÇOIS's *hair*] : My little boy. My poor little boy.

LUCIE : They made you scream, Henri, I heard you. You must feel ashamed.

HENRI : Yes.

LUCIE : I feel your shame with the same intensity. It's my shame, too. I told him I was alone and I was lying. With you I don't feel alone. [*To* CANORIS] You, you didn't scream. It's too bad.

CANORIS : I'm ashamed too.

LUCIE : Really! Why?

CANORIS : When Henri screamed I felt ashamed.

LUCIE : Just as well. Press close against me. I feel your arms and your shoulders, and the boy is heavy on my knees. That's good. Tomorrow I'll be quiet. Oh, how still I shall be! For him, for me, for Sorbier, for you. We are all one.

CURTAIN

A C T   I V

*Before the curtain goes up, a frightful voice is heard
singing "If all the cuckolds had bells." The curtain
rises on the schoolroom. It is the following morning.*
PELLERIN *is sitting on one of the benches, drinking.
He seems exhausted.* LANDRIEU, *in the teacher's chair,
is drinking; he is half drunk.* CLOCHET *is standing by
the window. He yawns; from time to time* LANDRIEU
bursts into laughter.

PELLERIN : What's so funny?

LANDRIEU [*cupping his hand around his ear*] : What?

PELLERIN : I asked you what you're laughing at.

LANDRIEU [*pointing to the radio and shouting*] : That.

PELLERIN : Eh?

LANDRIEU : Yes, I think it's a terrifically funny idea.

PELLERIN : What idea?

LANDRIEU : To put bells on cuckolds.

PELLERIN : Oh, hell! I didn't even hear it. [*He goes to
the radio set.*]

LANDRIEU [*shouting*] : Don't turn it off. [PELLERIN
turns it off. Silence.] You see, you see.

PELLERIN [*nonplussed*] : See what?

LANDRIEU : See the cold.

PELLERIN : You're cold in July?

LANDRIEU : I tell you it's cold; you don't understand
anything.

PELLERIN : What were you saying?

LANDRIEU : About what?

PELLERIN : About cuckolds.

LANDRIEU : Who said anything to you about cuckolds? Cuckold yourself. [*A pause.*] I'm going to get some news. [*He gets up and goes to the radio.*]

CLOCHET : There won't be any.

LANDRIEU : No news?

CLOCHET : Not at this hour.

LANDRIEU : We shall see, we shall see. [*He takes hold of the knob. Music, garbled stations.*]

PELLERIN : You're blasting our ears off.

LANDRIEU [*addressing the radio*] : Son of a bitch! [*A pause.*] To hell with it! I'm going to listen to the BBC; what's the wave length?

PELLERIN : Twenty-one meters.

[LANDRIEU *turns the dial: a speech in the Czech language.* LANDRIEU *begins to laugh.*]

LANDRIEU [*laughing*] : It's Czech, did you get that? At this very moment a Czech is speaking from London. Such a big world. [*He shakes the set.*] Can't you speak French? [*He turns the radio off.*] Give me a drink. [PELLERIN *pours him a glass of wine. He takes it from him and drinks.*] What are we farting around here for?

PELLERIN : Here or elsewhere—

LANDRIEU : I wish I were at the front.

PELLERIN : Aha!

LANDRIEU : Absolutely! That's where I'd like to be. [*He seizes him by the lapels of his jacket.*] And don't be telling me that I'm afraid to die.

PELLERIN : I didn't say anything.

LANDRIEU : What is death? Huh? What is it? 'Cause
we're going to have to find out, tomorrow, the day
after, or in three months.

CLOCHET [*vehemently*] : That's not true! It's not true!
The British will be pushed back into the sea.

LANDRIEU : Into the sea? You'll have 'em right up the
ass, the British. Right here in this village. It will be
biff-bam-zing, boom-diga-boom, bang on the town
hall, poom on the church. What will you be doing,
Clochet? You'll be in the basement! Ha! Ha! In the
cellar! It'll be fun. [*To* PELLERIN] Once you're dead
—I forget what I was going to say. Look, the little
wise guys upstairs—we're going to mow 'em down,
and that's no skin off my nose. Each in his turn.
That's what I tell myself. Today theirs. Tomorrow
mine. That's normal, isn't it? So am I normal. [*He
drinks.*] We're all fools. [*To* CLOCHET] Why are you
yawning?

CLOCHET : I'm bored.

LANDRIEU : Well, just drink up, then. Am I bored? But
you'd rather spy on us; you're making up your report
in your head. [*He pours a glass of wine and hands it
to* CLOCHET.] Drink up, come on, drink!

CLOCHET : I'm not allowed, I have a bad liver.

LANDRIEU : You'll drink this glass of wine or get it in
the face! [*A pause.* CLOCHET *extends his hand, takes
the glass, and drinks.*] Ha! ha! Fools, all fools, and it's
best that way.

[*Sound of steps; someone is pacing back and forth in
the attic overhead. All three look upwards. They listen in silence, then suddenly* LANDRIEU *wheels*

around, rushes to the door, opens it, and calls out]
Corbier! Corbier! [*A* TROOPER *appears.*] Go up and
quiet them. Let them have it. [*The* TROOPER *goes out.*
LANDRIEU *shuts the door and comes back to the
others; all three look upwards, listening. Silence.*]
We'll have to see their dirty mugs again. A lousy day.

PELLERIN : Do you need me to question them?

LANDRIEU : Why do you ask?

PELLERIN : I was thinking their chief might possibly be
hiding in the forest. I could take twenty men and beat
the brush.

LANDRIEU [*looking at him*] : Ah? [*A pause. The walking above continues.*] You'll stay here.

PELLERIN : All right. [*He shrugs his shoulders.*] We're
wasting our time.

LANDRIEU : That may be, but we'll waste it together.
[*They look up above, despite themselves, throughout the following conversation, until the sounds
overhead stop.*]

CLOCHET : It's time we brought the kid down.

LANDRIEU : I don't give a damn about the kid. I want to
make the big fellow open up.

PELLERIN : They won't talk.

LANDRIEU : I say they will. They're trash. You just have
to know how to handle them. Hell, we didn't rough
them up enough. [*A racket in the attic, then silence.*
LANDRIEU *is satisfied.*] What did I tell you? See,
they've calmed down. Nothing like a strong hand.
[*They are visibly relieved.*]

CLOCHET : All the same, you ought to begin with the
kid.

LANDRIEU : O.K. [*He goes to the door.*] Corbier! [*No reply.*] Corbier! [*Hurried steps in the corridor.* CORBIER *appears.*] Go fetch the kid.

CORBIER : The kid? They knocked him off.

LANDRIEU : What?

CORBIER : They knocked him off during the night. I found him with his head in his sister's lap. She said he was sleeping, but he was stone-dead. There were finger marks on his throat.

LANDRIEU : Oh? [*A pause.*] Who was walking around?

CORBIER : The Greek.

LANDRIEU : All right. You can go.

[CORBIER *goes out. Silence.* CLOCHET *gets up, and, despite himself, keeps looking toward the ceiling.*]

PELLERIN [*exploding*] : Fill them with lead, at once! Never see them again.

LANDRIEU : Shut up! [*He goes to the radio and turns it on. A slow waltz. Then he goes back to his chair and pours himself a drink. As he puts down his glass he notices Pétain's portrait.*] You see it, you see it all, but you wash your hands of it. You sacrifice yourself; you give yourself to France, but you don't give a damn for the dirty little details. You're part of history now, aren't you? And us, we're left in the shit. You dirty bastard! [*He throws his glass of wine at the picture.*]

CLOCHET : Landrieu!

LANDRIEU : Put that in your report. [*A pause. He calms himself with difficulty. He comes back to* PELLERIN.] It would be too easy to fill them with lead. That's what they want, don't you see that?

PELLERIN : Fine, if that's what they want, let's give it to them. But let's get rid of them, let's see the last of them.

LANDRIEU : I don't want them to kick off without having talked.

PELLERIN : They have nothing to tell us now. During the twenty-four hours they have been here their leader has had ample time to make his get-away.

LANDRIEU : I don't give a goddam about their leader. I want them to talk.

PELLERIN : And what if they don't?

LANDRIEU : Don't be difficult.

PELLERIN : But just the same, what if they don't talk?

LANDRIEU [*shouting*] : I told you not to knock yourself out over it.

PELLERIN : O.K., have them brought in.

LANDRIEU : Naturally I'll have them brought down.
[*But he doesn't budge.* CLOCHET *begins to laugh.*]

CLOCHET : What if they're martyrs, hey?
[LANDRIEU *suddenly goes to the door.*]

LANDRIEU : Bring them down.

CORBIER [*appearing*] : All three?

LANDRIEU : Yes, all three.
[CORBIER *goes out.*]

PELLERIN : You could have left the girl upstairs.
[*Footsteps overhead.*]

LANDRIEU : They are coming down. [*He goes to the radio and turns it off.*] If they surrender their chief, I'll let them go free.

CLOCHET : You're mad, Landrieu!

LANDRIEU : Shut your trap!

CLOCHET : They deserve death ten times over.

LANDRIEU : To hell with what they deserve. I want them to knuckle under. They won't pull that martyr stuff on me.

PELLERIN : I—look here, I couldn't take it. If I had to think they would live, that they might even survive us, and that all their lives they would remember us—

LANDRIEU : No need to get all upset. If they talk to save their necks now, they'll be avoiding that kind of memory afterwards. Here they are.

[PELLERIN *gets to his feet quickly and hides bottles and glasses under the chair. They are standing motionless as* LUCIE, HENRI, CANORIS, *and three* TROOPERS *enter. They look at each other in silence.*]

LANDRIEU : What have you done to the boy who was with you?

[*They do not answer.*]

PELLERIN : Murderers!

LANDRIEU : Shut up! [*To the others*] He wanted to talk, eh? And you wanted to prevent him.

LUCIE [*vehemently*] : That's not true. He didn't want to talk. Nobody would talk.

LANDRIEU : Well?

HENRI : He was too young. It was senseless to let him suffer.

LANDRIEU : Which of you strangled him?

CANORIS : We all decided on it and we are all responsible.

LANDRIEU : Very well. [*A pause.*] If you give us the information we want, I'll let you off.

CLOCHET : Landrieu!

LANDRIEU : I told you to be quiet. [*To the others*] Do

you accept? [*A pause.*] Well? Yes or no? [*They remain silent.* LANDRIEU *grows more and more upset.*] You refuse? You are ready to give three lives for one? That's absurd. [*A pause.*] It's life I am offering you! Life! Life! Are you deaf?

[*A pause. Then* LUCIE *takes a step toward them.*]

LUCIE : We've won! We've actually won! This moment pays us back for lots of things. All that I wanted to forget last night I'm proud to remember now. They tore off my dress. [*Pointing to* CLOCHET] He held my legs. [*Pointing to* LANDRIEU] He held my arms. [*Pointing to* PELLERIN] And he raped me. Now I can say it, I can yell it as loud as I please: you violated me and you are ashamed. I'm washed clean. Where are your pincers and pliers? Where are your whips? This morning you beg us to live. And our answer is no. No! You'll have to finish your job.

PELLERIN : That's enough! Enough I say! Let them have it!

LANDRIEU : Stop! Pellerin, I may not be in command here for much longer but while I am, my orders will not be questioned. Take them out.

CLOCHET : Can't we work on them a bit anyway? Because, after all, this is just talk. Nothing but talk. Hot air. [*Pointing to* HENRI] This guy came in yesterday cocky and swaggering and we made him scream like a girl.

HENRI : Just see if you can make me scream today.

LANDRIEU : Work on them if you have the courage to.

CLOCHET : Oh, the way I feel, even if they were martyrs

I wouldn't mind. I like the work for itself. [*To the* TROOPERS] Take them to the tables.

CANORIS : One moment. If we accept, how do we know that you'll let us live?

LANDRIEU : You have my word.

CANORIS : Yes. Well, I suppose that'll have to do. It's heads or tails. What will you do with us?

LANDRIEU : I'll turn you over to the German authorities.

CANORIS : Who will have us shot.

LANDRIEU : No. I'll explain your case.

CANORIS : Good. [*A pause.*] I'm disposed to talk, with my comrades' permission of course.

HENRI : Canoris!

CANORIS : Can I be alone with them? I think I can convince them.

LANDRIEU [*looking at him searchingly*] : Why do you want to talk now? Are you afraid to die?

[*A long silence. Then* CANORIS *bows his head.*]

CANORIS : Yes.

LUCIE : Coward!

LANDRIEU : Very well. [*To the* TROOPERS] You stand by the window. And you guard the door. Come along, men. [*To* CANORIS] You have a quarter of an hour to make up your mind.

[LANDRIEU, PELLERIN, *and* CLOCHET *leave by the rear door.*]

[*During the whole first part of the scene that follows,* LUCIE *remains silent and apparently uninterested in the discussion.*]

CANORIS [*goes to the window and then comes back. He*

speaks in low, vibrant tones] : The sun is overcast.
It is going to rain. Are you out of your senses? You
look at me as if I really intended to turn in our leader.
I simply mean to send them to the Servaz cave, as
Jean told us to do. [*A pause. He smiles.*] They've
damaged us a little, but we can still be very useful. [*A
pause.*] Come on. We have to talk. We can't squan-
der three lives. [*A pause. Gently*] Why are you so
bent on dying? What good will it do? Answer me!
What good will it do?

HENRI : No good.

CANORIS : Well, then?

HENRI : I'm tired.

CANORIS : Not as tired as I am. I'm fifteen years older
than you, and they've been rough on me. The life
they'll leave me is nothing to be desired.

HENRI [*gently*] : Are you so afraid of dying?

CANORIS : I'm not afraid. I lied to them just now; I'm
not afraid. But we have no right to die for nothing.

HENRI : And why not? Why not? They broke my
wrists, they tore open my flesh: haven't I paid for
the right to die? We've won. Why do you ask me
to begin life again when I can die at peace with myself?

CANORIS : Because there are comrades who need our
help.

HENRI : What comrades? Where?

CANORIS : Everywhere.

HENRI : Oh, you think so! If they spare our lives, they'll
send us to the salt mines.

CANORIS : Well, you can always escape.

HENRI : You think you'll escape? You're only a shadow of what you were.

CANORIS : If I can't, then you will.

HENRI : One chance in a hundred.

CANORIS : The chance is worth taking. And even if we don't escape, there'll be other men in the mines: old men who are sick, women who are at the end of their strength. They need us.

HENRI : Listen, when I saw the kid lying on the floor, so pale and white, I thought: all right, I've done what I've done and I regret nothing. But of course I was sure that I'd be shot at dawn. If I hadn't thought that six hours later I'd be lying on the same dungheap— [*Shouting*] I don't want to survive him. I don't want to survive the kid for thirty years. Canoris, it will be so easy; we won't even have time to look at the muzzles of their guns.

CANORIS : We have no right to die for nothing.

HENRI : Can you still see sense in living when there are men who beat you until they break your bones? It is so dark now. [*He looks out of the window.*] You're right, it is going to rain.

CANORIS : The sky is completely overcast. It will be a good shower.

HENRI [*abruptly*] : It was out of pride.

CANORIS : What?

HENRI : The kid. I think I killed him out of pride.

CANORIS : Why dwell on that? He had to die.

HENRI : I'll drag that doubt around like a ball and chain. Every minute of my life I'll suspect myself. [*A pause.*] I can't do it! I can't live.

CANORIS : What heroics! You'll have more than enough to keep you busy helping others; you'll forget yourself. You're too concerned with yourself, Henri; you want to redeem your life. Hell, what you need to do is work, and you'll be saving your life into the bargain. [*A pause.*] Look here, Henri, if you die today, the picture will be completed; then you'll really have killed him out of pride, it will be settled forever. But if you live—

HENRI : Then what?

CANORIS : Then nothing will be settled. It's by your whole life that your individual acts will be judged. [*A pause.*] If you let yourself be shot while there's still work for you to do, nothing will be more senseless than your death. [*A pause.*] Shall I call them?

HENRI [*pointing to* LUCIE] : Let her decide.

CANORIS : Do you hear, Lucie?

LUCIE : Decide what? Oh yes. Well, it's all settled: tell them that we won't talk and let them make it quick.

CANORIS : What about the comrades, Lucie?

LUCIE : I have no comrades now. [*She goes up to the* TROOPERS.] Go get them. We'll tell them nothing.

CANORIS [*following her, to the* TROOPERS] : We still have five minutes. Wait. [*He leads her back to the front of the stage.*]

LUCIE : Yes, five minutes. And do you expect to convince me in five minutes?

CANORIS : Yes.

LUCIE : You simple soul! Yes, yes, you can live, your conscience is clear. They've roughed you up a bit, that's all. But me, they've humiliated me so that there's not a morsel of my flesh that's not detestable to me. [*To* HENRI] And you who carry on so because you strangled a boy, have you forgotten that the boy was my brother and that I didn't say a word? I've taken all the guilt on myself; they must get rid of me and all the guilt with me. Go ahead. Live, if you can accept yourselves. But I hate myself and after my death I want it to be as if I had never existed.

HENRI: I won't abandon you, Lucie, and I shall do whatever you decide. [*A pause.*]

CANORIS: Then I shall have to save you despite yourselves.

LUCIE: You'll talk?

CANORIS: There's no other way.

LUCIE [*violently*]: I'll tell them that you're lying, that you made the whole thing up. [*A pause.*] If I'd known that you would knuckle under I'd never have let you lay a finger on my brother.

CANORIS: Your brother wanted to denounce Jean and I want to send them on a false trail.

LUCIE: It's the same thing. They'll have the same look of triumph in their eyes.

CANORIS: Lucie! So it was out of pride that you let François die?

LUCIE: You are wasting your breath if you think you can make me feel remorse.

A TROOPER: You have two minutes.

CANORIS: Henri!

HENRI: I'll abide by her decision.

CANORIS [*to* LUCIE]: What do you care about these men? In six months they'll hole up in some cellar and

the first grenade tossed into it will write finish to
the whole story. It's all the rest that counts. The
world and what you can do in it, our comrades and
what you can do for them.

LUCIE : I've been wrung dry. I feel entirely alone. I can
think only of myself.

CANORIS [*gently*] : You really would miss nothing on
earth?

LUCIE : Nothing. Everything is spoiled.

CANORIS : Well— [*A gesture of resignation. He takes
a step toward the* TROOPERS. *The rain begins to fall;
first light and scanty, then a heavy downpour.*]

LUCIE [*sharply*] : What's that? [*In low, slow tones*]
The rain. [*She goes to the window and watches the
downpour. A pause.*] It's three months since I heard
the sound of rain. [*A pause.*] My God, all these past
days the weather has been perfect; it was horrible.
I couldn't remember what bad weather is like, I
thought we should always have to live under the
sun. [*A pause.*] It's coming down hard, it's going to
smell like wet grass. [*Her lips tremble.*] I don't want
to—I don't want to— [HENRI *and* CANORIS *come close
to her.*]

HENRI : Lucie!

LUCIE : I don't want to cry, I'll become silly. [HENRI
takes her in his arms.] Let me go! [*Shouting*] I
loved life, I loved life! [*She sobs on* HENRI's *shoulder.*]

TROOPER [*approaching*] : Well? Time's up.

CANORIS [*after a glance at* LUCIE] : Go tell your su-
periors that we'll talk.

[*The* TROOPER *goes out. A pause.*]

LUCIE [*collecting herself*] : Is it true? Are we going to live? I was already on the other side. Look at me. Smile at me. It's so long since I've seen anyone smile. Have we done right, Canoris? Have we really done right?

CANORIS : We're doing what is right. We must live.

[LANDRIEU, PELLERIN, CLOCHET *enter.*]

LANDRIEU : Well?

CANORIS : On the road to Grenoble, at the forty-second boundary-mark, take the path to your right. Fifty or sixty yards in the woods, you'll find a thicket and behind the thicket a cave. Our leader is hidden there with arms.

LANDRIEU [*to the* TROOPERS] : Ten men. Send them off immediately. Try to bring him back alive. [*A pause.*] Take the prisoners back upstairs.

[*The* TROOPERS *hustle the prisoners out.* CLOCHET, *after a moment's hesitation, slips out after them.*]

PELLERIN : Do you think they told us the truth?

LANDRIEU : Of course. They're fools. [*He sits behind the desk.*] Well, we've finally had them. You saw their exit? They were less cocky than when they came in. [CLOCHET *enters. Amiably*] Well, Clochet, we've had them, haven't we?

CLOCHET [*rubbing his hands nervously*] : Yes, yes, we've had them.

PELLERIN [*to* LANDRIEU] : Are you going to let them live?

LANDRIEU : Oh, for the present anyway. [*A volley outside.*] What's that?

[CLOCHET *laughs nervously, hiding his face with his hand.*] Clochet, you didn't—

[CLOCHET *nods in the affirmative and keeps on laughing.*]

CLOCHET : I thought it would be more human.

LANDRIEU : You bastard! [*A second volley. He runs to the window.*]

PELLERIN : Let it go now; never two without three.

LANDRIEU : I don't want—

PELLERIN : Could any of us face the one survivor?

CLOCHET : In another minute no one will ever again think of all this. No one but us.

[*A third volley.* LANDRIEU *collapses in his chair.*]

LANDRIEU : Damn!

[CLOCHET *goes to the radio and turns it on. Music.*]

CURTAIN

A Note on the Type

IN WHICH THIS BOOK IS SET

This book was set on the Linotype in Janson, a recutting made direct from the type cast from matrices (now in possession of the Stempel foundry, Frankfurt am Main) made by Anton Janson some time between 1660 and 1687.

Of Janson's origin nothing is known. He may have been a relative of Justus Janson, a printer of Danish birth who practiced in Leipzig from 1614 to 1635. Some time between 1657 and 1668 Anton Janson, a punch-cutter and type-founder, bought from the Leipzig printer Johann Erich Hahn the type-foundry which had formerly been a part of the printing house of M. Friedrich Lankisch. Janson's types were first shown in a specimen sheet issued at Leipzig about 1675. Janson's successor, and perhaps his son-in-law, Johann Karl Edling, issued a specimen sheet of Janson types in 1689. His heirs sold the Janson matrices in Holland to Wolffgang Dietrich Erhardt, of Leipzig.

COMPOSED AND PRINTED BY
Vail-Ballou Press, Inc., BINGHAMTON, N.Y.
BOUND BY
H. Wolff, NEW YORK.